HARD

WISDOM

FROM THE SCHOOL OF

HARD

KNOCKS

ALAIN BURRESE

HOW TO AVOID A FIGHT AND THINGS TO DO WHEN YOU CAN'T OR DON'T WANT TO

Authors Choice Press

San Jose New York Lincoln Shanghai

Hard-Won Wisdom From the School of Hard Knocks
How to Avoid a Fight and Things To Do When You Can't or Don't Want To

Authors Choice Press
an imprint of iUniverse.com, Inc.

For information address:
iUniverse.com, Inc.
5220 S 16th, Ste. 200
Lincoln, NE 68512
www.iuniverse.com

Originally published by Paladin Press

Cover photo from "Hapkido Hoshinsul,"
Paladin Press copyright 1999. Used by permission.

The information presented in this book is for reference and information purposes only! The author, publisher, and distributors do not in any way endorse or condone any illegal activity or act that may be depicted in the following pages. Therefore, the author, publisher, and distributors disclaim any liability and assume no responsibility for the use or misuse of the information herein.

ISBN: 0-595-17422-1

Printed in the United States of America

CONTENTS

WARNING

The information presented in this book is *for reference and information purposes only*! The author, publisher, and distributors do not in any way endorse or condone any illegal activity or act that may be depicted in the following pages. Therefore, the author, publisher, and distributors disclaim *any* liability and assume no responsibility for the use or misuse of the information herein.

WHUMP!

Yes, that's a wall. And that's the sound your body makes hitting the wall at high speed. Well, you ninny, I thought, you did ask to see his favorite technique, so don't be surprised that you just got ricocheted off the wall.

These are the sorts of intelligent thoughts that passed through my head as I tried to keep my eyeballs from clicking together inside my skull after encountering a much more solid mass than I at entirely too high a speed.

"You can put me down now," I grunted.

Alain released his grip and stepped

back. No wonder this gorilla has survived so many brawls in the military, I thought. He was fast, strong, and his favorite move was both simple and brutally effective. It also left room for negotiation with the guy (me, in this case) once the guy's teeth stopped rattling. (And no, I'm not going to tell you what the move is.)

"Okay, do it again," I told him.

This time it was Alain who slammed against the wall—his eyes wide as he flew by. (Hey, I didn't say I was just going to stand there, did I?)

"That's the counter to that move," I told him. "If you ever feel things going wrong like that, stop immediately and do something else."

Unlike many people who, when their favorite move goes wrong, try to force it, Alain didn't. He adapted immediately and took it in. The next time I tried the counter, he countered again and we ended up springing back from each other—no damage done, but neither of us remained in the other's range either.

This is the sign of a good fighter: someone who knows when to backpedal because things aren't going right. Kid's been there, I thought. He instinctively knows things can go wrong in a fight, and he's fast enough mentally to adjust. This is one dangerous dude.

Alain and I come from totally different backgrounds. He's a Montana country boy who grew up watching elk walk across his yard. A far cry from the streets of Los Angeles. But because of that, in many ways Alain is more in tune with the real world and how most people still fight. He comes from a place where it's *mano y mano*—knock-down, drag-out brawls. Which I've come to realize is how much of the world still works outside the depths of the city streets. It's not all running gang wars and weapons out there (not yet), and hopefully it never will be.

VIII

The 82d Airborne convinced him that there's no such thing as a perfectly good airplane, and the smartest thing you can do is jump out of one (a point he and I still disagree on). Then it was on to Korea for sniper training and eventually teaching. Along the way, there was a thunderin' herd of barroom and barracks brawls.

Alain thrived in this environment, and the lessons and wisdom he gained from this kind of fighting are invaluable. His is a life-style that isn't street but is indeed dangerous. It's that risky middle ground that most people are likely to find themselves on. This isn't deep in the realm of biker bars, but it is the sort of trouble you'll run into in your local college watering hole, at a stop light, or even outside the supermarket. In short, it's exactly the sort of circumstances most people find themselves in when it comes to violence.

The reason this middle ground is risky is that it can easily float into the more extreme territory, and unless you know what to look for, you'll never figure out which is which.

You can get in as much trouble by landing too hard on someone as you can by not landing hard enough on someone else. The guy who jumps out of his car and comes running up to you at a stop light for you cutting him off probably doesn't have a weapon, but you still may end up in a punchfest with him.

I've encountered many a martial artist who told me, "If I ever had to use it, I'd go totally killer on him." Not a good idea. Yes, violence can and will escalate into those nasty situations. Unfortunately a whole lot of whether they do or not depends on your not going into kung fu killer mode. Do it when it's right; don't do it if it isn't necessary. The guy who's running at you probably doesn't have a weapon, but he might.

That's where this book comes in. It is a very good tool for finding and identifying the middle ground between civilized society and the depths of criminal/gang/street violence. In short, it's exactly what most people are going to be running into out there. What's most likely for most people is the occasional drunk or obnoxious clown who's looking for trouble and might just decide to pick you. You need to be able to distinguish him from the total psychopath with an Uzi.

Read and learn from this book. It covers a much-overlooked area of the subject of fighting: the middle ground.

—Marc "Animal" MacYoung

Acknowledgments

There are many people who have contributed throughout the years to the writing of this book. Most of them are friends I've run with, gotten into trouble with, gotten out of trouble with, and so on. I'd like to acknowledge and thank a few of them here in no particular order.

Frank Spears, sniper. You went through hell twice to earn that title and are always there when needed. Thanks buddy.

Brian Hurd, one of the original three in Korea. I wish you well in all you're doing now.

Jeff Stephenson, 82nd Airborne. The Airborne boxer. Here's to you and the Bottoms Up Club. Those were the days.

Rhett Kurkowski, 82nd Airborne, Ranger. Were we crazy at times, or what? All my best, guy.

Dave Wojciechowski, the wizard. A true friend if ever there was one. Thanks for everything, and may you always be blessed.

John Steffes, 82nd Airborne. My squash partner in Korea with the 2nd ID. Happy hunting and fishing, with whatever you're after.

Eric Allen, Airborne, Ranger, sniper. Wishing you the best always.

Greg Baker, Airborne, Ranger, sniper. It was fun working and playing wasn't it? Wishing you the perfect wave; aloha, dude.

Marc "Animal" MacYoung, a true warrior. Your books inspired and taught, but you've done more. Thanks, you're a good man.

Robert L. Burrese, my father. Without you when I was young, I wouldn't have walked. Without you when a teenager, I probably would have landed in jail. Without you, I wouldn't be the man I am today. I hope I make you proud.

To all the others that I trained with, under, and around. We had some good times throughout the years, I'm glad we can look back and laugh. Take care, and may you each be blessed in your own particular way.

INTRODUCTION

Have you ever been sitting around with the guys and someone starts a story with, "Remember the time when . . .?" Well, I've spent many hours in these sessions, and many of them turn to tales of fights, brawls, and general mayhem. Often you hear things like, "I learned never to do that again" and "I'll tell you, when you stomp on a guy with these mothers on, he doesn't get up." And so they go, with each person contributing lessons learned and antidotes to amuse and inform his companions.

That's what this book is about. It's not a book to teach you how to become some martial arts master. And it's not a how-to book on squishing folks like bugs. I won't be explaining a bunch of techniques for you to practice and use in certain situations. This book is written as if you and I were sitting and having a drink as we swapped stories and told each other what we've learned about fighting and such, and how we learned the lessons.

I don't know everything about fighting; nobody does. But because of my hot temper, I used to get into my share of scraps and brawls. To tell the truth, for a while I liked it. Spending two years in the 82nd Airborne Division and another 18 months as a sniper in Tong Du Chong, South Korea, gave me ample opportunity to practice my "squash." (A buddy, John, and I used to call each other "squash partners." We got it from the Clint Eastwood movie *Any Which Way You Can*.)

Yes, I have had some formal training in a couple classical martial arts. I used to compete in judo, and I have studied karate, tae kwon do, and hapkido at different times. I have also done extensive studying on the different aspects of the martial way, and I have applied these teachings to training and life.

So I'm going to talk about a lot of different aspects of fighting and violence. Naturally, a lot of it will be about things to do and, just as important, what not to do. But I'll also talk about other related considerations: why fights happen, when you should fight, when you shouldn't, and so on. I'll talk quite a bit about avoiding fights and staying out of trouble, because I've learned that there are many better things to do with yourself. What has really amazed me is how often the same principles work in other areas of one's life. Also, conversely, I've applied things I've learned in other areas to increase my ability to survive dangerous situations.

Much of what I'm going to be saying is pretty general, and they're things I have found to be true in many circumstances. I'll be relaying a lot of stories about actual physical encounters that either I or close friends of mine were in. I'll tell you what happened and what can be learned from each experience.

The other main source of information comes from my father, who did his share of fighting when he was younger. He taught me much about fighting as well as other lessons of life. Most of all, he taught me the power of a person's determination and will—key ingredients in determining the victor of a physical encounter as well as most of life.

One of the most knowledgeable authors I have found for practical advice on staying alive in hostile environments is Marc "Animal" MacYoung. I will mention him periodically, and if some of my stuff sounds like some of his, it's because I have been influenced by his writing and teaching. I give him a lot of credit for some of the things I know. I read his first book, *Cheap Shots, Ambushes, and Other Lessons*, while I was stationed in South Korea. I wasn't new to the game, so as I read it I found myself saying, "This guy knows what he's talking about." Rather than just read his books and then stow them away on a shelf, I started to apply some of the things he wrote about. I practiced some of his stuff and looked for the situations he talked about in the bars I was frequenting. That's the key to any instructional book. You need to apply the things you read about. So as you read this book, take the lessons and see how they fit into your own life and circumstances. Of course, there may be numerous lessons learned in one encounter, so I may refer to stories told in different chapters once in a while, rather than tell the same story twice.

I prefer to get in close and do a lot of grabbing and slamming, so I won't be talking at great length about the applications of high spinning back kicks. I really like Rowdy Roddy Piper movies, because many of his fight scenes are like watching home movies. He does some of the professional wrestling stuff, but he does a lot of the tackling and slamming and jamming that is similar to the way I used to get the job done. The things that have worked for me are not the only ways to do this. Like the old saying, there's more than one way to skin a platypus.

I've tried to pick experiences that teach a wide number of important factors dealing with fights and combat. There are things I won't tell, just like you have your own skeletons. And at times I may seem to be changing sides. This is because nothing is constant. We are all changing, and as I've changed and grown up, my thoughts and actions have changed too.

So take my experiences and learn from them what you can. Laugh at my stupidity in areas, and think of how you can prevent yourself from making the same mistakes. Learn from the things that have worked for me; they may work well for you also.

I'm still learning too, so I'd like to tell you something my father told me, which my grandfather told him: "Learn from my mistakes and don't do the same. Go out and make your own, then come back and tell me about it so we both learn."

A LITTLE ABOUT THE GAME

"All they that take the sword,

shall perish with the sword"

—New Testament

Matthew 26:52

The title of this section of the book isn't very accurate, because most fights between adults are not a game. Serious consequences happen when people fight. People get hurt and people get killed. Some of the injuries will last a lifetime, and that's when you're lucky enough to still have a life. Many wind up behind bars, and unlike in *Jailhouse Rock*, it's not fun spending time in prison on a manslaughter charge for killing a guy in a fistfight. The good thing about that movie is that it shows you how easy it can happen. Elvis got into a scrap, and before he knew it the guy was dead. Fights often break out that quickly, and people die that easily.

5

There was an incident in Portland when a guy called another guy outside. The one doing the talking was a young punk showing how tough he was; the other guy was a little older and didn't really want to mess with the young buck. But enough was enough and he stepped outside. The fight lasted all of a couple seconds. The older guy kicked the younger man in the chest, and the punk went down, smashing his head on the pavement. I don't know if it was the blow to the chest or the head, or a combination of the two, but he died and the older guy was arrested. It happens, and most old-timers have seen this kind of thing across the nation.

So in this section I'm going to talk a little about violence and fighting. Then I'll take a look at the key to surviving almost everything in life, not just in the martial realm. The most important self-defense tool you have is your awareness. Then I'll ramble a bit about losing, because it can and will happen; 50 percent of those who fight lose. Sure, you want to be in the upper 50 that wins, but it doesn't always work out that way. And when it does, sometimes you have the law to answer to.

VIOLENCE AND FIGHTING IN GENERAL

CHAPTER 1

War is like love; it always finds a way."

—Bertolt Brecht

Mother Courage

"Violent acts have been occurring and fights have been fought for as long as people have been running around. When we look at the animal kingdom we see the same. However, animals often have better reasons to engage in their violent activities than we do. They usually fight over food or territorial rights. Humans, on the other hand, fight about all kinds of stupid things. It's usually over the ego of one or more of the individuals involved. These are your typical barroom brawls that happen all over the world.

Most of these "ego" fights can be avoided and don't really have any good reason to be fought. But then we have another area of violence. It's a sad and unfortunate fact that some people prey on other people. Most of

7

the time they prey on the weak. It's difficult to follow any form of news anymore without hearing about some sociopath that has initiated a violent attack on an unsuspecting victim. These forms of violence can often be avoided, but in a little different manner. One must increase his awareness level and be on the lookout for possible situations to steer clear of, rather than just walking away from a loudmouth in a bar to avoid an ego clash.

So in this chapter, I'm going to give you a few thoughts on some different areas dealing with violent encounters, fights, and other related subjects.

FIGHTS

First, let's look at the common bar fight that is ever so popular in the movies as well as in saloons around the country. We can always see it coming when our hero goes into the local drinking establishment. We wait for this part of the movie and rewind it on video. Magazines have ranked the best bar fights in the movies, and we've all found ourselves discussing our all-time favorites. (One of my all-time favorite movie fights is the bathroom fight in *The Warriors*. Watch this and ask yourself if it really looks like fun.)

The funny thing is, you can often see these encounters arising in real life, too. Many of your common bar fights start in similar ways, and they are usually over the same things. It was like this when my dad was younger, and it's like this now. It will probably be like this long after we're gone. (Pay attention to the avoidance stuff real close if you want this to be a lot later rather than sooner.)

So why do most of these "stupid" fights occur? I call them stupid fights because they are more retarded than the other kinds of violence I'll talk about. Usually it's testosterone combined with a little alcohol. "He looked at me funny," or "He's eyeing your woman, man." Then the two confront each other and start throwing out words, and after it heats up a bit, punches are thrown. You can usually see this starting from the first looks, and a good bouncer will smooth it out at this point and not let it escalate to actual physical violence.[1]

After punches start flying, things start looking a lot different from the movies. Usually things happen in a big blur and it's pretty ugly. No fancy martial arts moves and flying kicks here. Even guys who practice that flashy stuff in the dojo revert back to the real simple animalistic things that work in the street. Namely, going ballistic on a guy until he drops. Most of these fights are over real quick. You don't have two guys knocking each other back and forth across the bar for 15 minutes like in the climax of so many cinema attractions. (I always wondered about this. Why can the hero knock out so many people throughout the movie in a second or two, but it takes him 10 or 15 minutes to finish off the main bad guy at the end?)

Fights like this used to break out in the barracks I lived in while in the army and in the dorms I worked and lived in while going to college. Again, most of these incidents started over someone's ego being hurt. Maybe he was just drunk, mad, or both and looking for trouble. Whatever it was, or is, when you get into a fight here, everyone knows who you are. It's a whole different set of rules. You hurt a guy seriously here and you're going to get slammed. You can't run and hide.

Another thing, it might be a friend of yours. "What?" you ask. It's pretty common for little fights to break out to show who's "the boss." I was in a number of these while I was in the service. After someone shows the other who the boss is, it's over, and hard feelings usually aren't kept very long. You see this kind of fight in the movies; after the two slug it out, they go have a beer with each other.

These are the kinds of fights I've witnessed the most and participated in far too often. When I was younger, I was quick to let fly if a guy said the wrong thing to me. Dumb!

Yes, these were unnecessary fights, and I was a big part of the stupidity. Even though many of these kinds of fights aren't as serious as other forms of violent physical encounters, people still become maimed, hurt, killed, and sent to prison. Sometimes serious injuries are unintentional, but it's a little too late after the damage is done. Do you want to spend time behind bars over the way someone looked at you or because of accidentally hurting someone more than you intended? I sure as hell don't!

VIOLENT PHYSICAL ASSAULT

I classify this a little differently from your typical fight. This is more like a person preying on someone else. The savage atrocities that plague our society bombard us every time we turn around. Just recently, while I was visiting my grandparents in Helena, Montana, I read a front-page story about an 83-year-old woman who had been raped. At 3:30 in the afternoon, a man forced her into her house as she was opening the door when returning home. He raped her and left an hour later. My grandmother, who is also 83, commented, "What's going on in this world? You would think an old woman like me wouldn't have to worry about that kind of thing anymore."

Physical assault includes many things, including muggings, rapes, and the new "thrill kills" or assaults. These aren't so much "macho" as they are someone preying on another human being. This peril has existed throughout time and is ever so prominent today. Awareness is the primary self-defense tool for these situations. But I do feel that physical training can help certain people to come out of these situations with minimum suffering. I say certain people, because without the proper mind-set needed to inflict injury on another human being, all the physical training in the world will do you no good.

VIOLENCE AND DOMINATION

The desire to dominate another person or a race of people has been around for ages. In Fredrick Lovret's *The Way and the Power*, he quotes Genghis Khan: "There is no joy a man can feel which is greater than when he destroys his enemies and drives them before him." It is not the act of war or fighting, but the feeling of worth after winning that becomes addicting. If you have ever won at anything, you can relate to this. The problem is, some people can only feel this way by dominating and controlling others. It's sad that they have such a low self-worth that they must resort to this behavior.

Don't confuse this with the person who feels the thrill of victory after a battle because he knew he gave his all and came out victorious. There is a huge difference. I'm talking about bullies, wife and child beaters, and the like. These people have such a shallow sense of self-worth that they must dominate someone weaker to feel important. This is sick in my book, and unfortunately, most of these people need to be met with physical violence to counter them. You need to stand up to a bully or call the police against an abuser. This, of course, will only stop their immediate actions, but it will take a lot more to cure the sickness that causes these people to act this way in the first place. Some cases are more severe than others, and a bully may be cured by getting knocked on the ground. But the underlying sense of self-worth still needs to be helped for this person to grow as a person.

SERIOUSNESS

Yes, there is a long history of violence, and it probably won't stop; in fact, it looks at times as if it's getting worse. Many people don't understand violence and fighting at all. It is completely foreign to them. Others lead a life full of it. Some, like

11

me, have walked a bit on both sides. Having seen both sides, I want to leave the violent side behind. Sure, I'm prepared if something comes my way, but I'll try to avoid an encounter first. Fighting is serious.

Think about the things in this book and how they relate to the life-style you choose. It's your choice as to how you want to live. It is my sincerest hope that the information in this book will help you realize that fighting is a no-win situation. I hope you are prepared to defend yourself in the event it is necessary, especially if your occupation demands it. But don't read this book to use the information to harm others needlessly. Fighting should always be your last option. It's serious.

NOTES

1. A bouncer's job isn't to fight and beat people up. It's to keep the establishment from being ruined and to ensure the safety of all people in the joint. The best way to do this is to stop confrontations *before* they become physical. Of course, this isn't possible 100 percent of the time, but the best bouncers fight the least.

ANYONE CAN BE BEAT

CHAPTER 2

"Revenge belongs to God."

—Gen. George S. Patton

"Live by the sword, die by the sword" is an old maxim, and one that is often true. If you fight enough, several things are bound to happen, none of them good. At the end of one of those fights you may find yourself on the ground seriously hurt or, worse yet, dead. Neither is something any of us go out looking for, but it could easily happen.

On the other hand, you may have done the serious hurting or killing. Then you have the law to deal with, and you could easily end up behind bars. Personally, there are too many things I would rather be doing than sitting in a cell because I punched a guy in

13

the throat and crushed his windpipe. All because he looked at me funny from across the bar.

Anyway, right now we are discussing being beat. If you already know how to stomp folks, you don't have to worry about losing so you can skip this chapter, right? Wrong! *I don't care how good you are, you can be taken out!* The old saying, "There's always someone better" is true, but you can also be beat by someone less skilled and weaker. Anyone can get lucky. There's also sucker punchers out there who only need you to let your guard down for a minute and WHAM!

I'm telling you, the longer you lead a life that involves cracking skulls, the greater the possibility that you'll get yours busted open one day. It's simple arithmetic—is a boxer with a 3–0 record as impressive as one with a 30–0 record? Of course not! It's much more difficult to go 30 fights without losing than to win 3. That's why there are so few boxers who retire undefeated. Will you hang your head in shame the next time you frequent the bar because you got whipped? Or will you be lying in a hospital racking up medical bills worth your next 10 years' salary? Or will you be six feet under? If you fight enough, sooner or later you will lose. The severity of the beating will be the only variable.

There are no certainties in any physical encounter. I was asked by a guy, who had far less experience than I, if he threw a sucker punch out of the blue, would I automatically be able to block it and take him out. I answered truthfully, "Not necessarily." I then told him, "Anyone can be taken out by anyone in the right situation. "I was living in Japan at the time, so I was able to illustrate this fact by looking at the country's popular sport, sumo. Every so often, one of the smaller and lesser-ranked wrestlers beats one of the top dogs.

I wouldn't want to face "Animal" MacYoung one-on-one in an alley with a knife. He teaches the stuff! Even so, I could get lucky and my tanto would do a lot of damage if it connected.

But why would I want to go toe-to-toe with someone better than me? I'd be a lot better off sneaking up on him and ambushing him when he was off guard. True, this would be more difficult to do to Marc than to most people, but I am a sniper and was trained to get in and out of places without being detected. Speaking of which, why would I, a sniper, want to take on a knife fighting instructor with a knife? I'd be much better off taking him out from 600 meters or more with a 7.62-caliber rifle. Sure, he's good with a blade, but a knife just doesn't cut it in a gunfight, especially at 600 or more meters.[1]

Do you see the kind of thinking here? Yes, there's always someone better, and you may meet him one day. But you can also be beat by someone who isn't as good but evens the odds by using different weapons, ambushes, friends, or just plain getting lucky. And with guns—any guns—the odds are with the wielder of the weapon.

Even if you are proficient at so-called gun disarmament techniques, you can be shot and killed by someone inexperienced with a gun. You have to be very close to the person with the gun to be able to take it from him, and even then you're likely to take a bullet while doing it. (Or someone else nearby may take a round as the weapon discharges when being taken away.)

You see, guns are the great equalizer. The 110-pound weakling doesn't have to work out and develop a body like Arnold Schwarzenegger's to get even with the guy kicking sand in his face. All he needs to do is buy a firearm. Times are changing and so are physical confrontations. More and more, you need to worry about the other person packing a weapon.

Not too long ago I was talking with some friends back in Montana. Todd, one of the participants in the conversation, was home on leave from the Marine Corps. Now Todd's a big guy and can handle himself, but he was talking about some of the things you had to be concerned with down in

15

southern California where he was stationed. "You might have a young punk kid come up and demand money or whatever. It could be a kid that you could backhand into the dirt, but he's packing a gun. And they will use them!" So, a big bad tough guy can get blown away by a little punk with a 9mm. Nobody is bulletproof!

I guess the reason I'm beating this topic to death (pardon the pun) is because it's important. Too many people don't realize this until it's too late, and even when people do know it, they think it applies to everyone but them. Somehow they are immune to these universal truths. (People tend to think this way about many things, not just fighting.) This "it can't happen to me" attitude can be very dangerous to one's health. At times I get this attitude about things and have to do a reality check to bring me back to my senses. Truth is, *it can't happen to you until it does.*

So why am I writing about losing, anyway? This is a book about protecting oneself and how to stay alive long enough to collect a pension. It's a book about not getting beat, so why write about getting stomped? Well, here's a story.

John was one of my running buddies in South Korea. Both of us were sort of carrying on family traditions of busting heads. While others told stories about John and I, we would tell stories about our fathers and the battles they had waged when they were younger. Both were fighters and both were good.

It was while we were in South Korea that John received the news that his father had been killed. It turned out that a guy had ambushed him in a parking lot one night while he was picking up his brother. Knowing that he couldn't take him face -to-face, the guy decided to blindside him with a metal pipe to the head.

I'm sure John's father could have taken the guy out, even with the pipe, in a fair fight.[2] But on that night, the guy got lucky and was able to ambush John's dad and get in with the pipe before he had a chance to react.

I'm not sure why his guard was down. Maybe he was tired; maybe his mind was on other things. Or maybe the guy was an experienced ambusher. They do exist out there. For whatever reason, John's dad lost his life to a cheap shot with a metal pipe from out of the dark.

The guy who did it went to prison, but that didn't help John or his family much. Death hurts those left alive more than those who have departed. I saw firsthand how John took his father's death. John and his dad were very close, and it was made worse by the way it had happened. But we didn't stop to think about it at the time. Actually, John might have fought a little more because of this, something I understand wholeheartedly. It was only later, when I really started to think about fighting and violence and working on bettering myself in areas beyond just fists, that I realized the significance of John's father's death. If he could be killed like that, so could John. If John could be killed that easily, well, so could I. And so can anyone else out there.

Here's the stupid thing: even after this happened, John and I kept on fighting. And we still fought over idiotic things that could have been avoided.

So stop a moment and think about how easy it would be for someone to ambush you, or maybe slip in a sucker punch with devastating results. There are a lot of good reasons for living, and losing your life in a fight isn't worth the stupid things many fights are over.

I've had a few talks with Animal about some of the people he's known who were "good" but are no longer around. The pain is compounded by the haunting memories of everyone else you've buried.

With this topic, let's talk a little about revenge, since that's what fuels many ambushes. Revenge can be real ugly. Remember, every time you fight, it may only be a battle in a larger war. After you beat someone, you need to be careful that they don't come back looking to even the score or maybe get ahead. Worse, you may have his friends or family after you. Personally, we've (all the people I've run with) always had this code of honor that if it was a one-on-one, the rest would stay out of it. I always told people to stay out unless I was about to be killed. Then they could break it up and carry me home. This was the agreement we had.

Others don't always play by these gentleman rules. I've learned this firsthand. You could be facing a whole gang of friends after a one-on-one, or they may just join in during the fight. They may not wait for you to even start winning. Worse yet, a guy you beat may catch you alone and unarmed with half a dozen of his friends with baseball bats a month or two later. You may have forgotten the incident, but he's been plotting his revenge ever since.

A friend of mine, a fellow sniper instructor, once taught a young private how to blow up a car in a booby traps class. Anyway, this guy went back to the States on leave and got himself into trouble with some guy over a girl. The young private got stomped pretty good by this guy. He knew he couldn't get even in a fight, so he waited until right before returning to South Korea and blew up the guy's car. When the kid got back to South Korea he was still a mess from the beating he took, but he was happy that he blew his rival's car all over the yard one early morning. No one was hurt, but it's something to think about the next time you smash and stomp someone into the ground. There's a reason why so much has been said about revenge throughout history.

So, what can we learn from this? The more fighting you do, the more you have to be on the lookout for those seeking revenge. After a fight when John and I sent two big tankers to the hospital (see Chapter 15 for details), we were told that they said they would be looking for us. Always cocky, John replied,

"Hey, if they're stupid enough to come back for more, we'll do it again." But we both raised our levels of awareness for a while. (Like they weren't high enough already, sheesh!)

Did you catch that? Even though both John and I had pretty high awareness levels all the time, we were a little extra cautious and on the lookout for those two and friends. My father also warned us when I told him what happened in a letter. He said to keep an eye out, for those kind will come back with ambushes, weapons, and help.

So we raised our awareness, but only for a while. Six months later, the only time we thought of those two was when stories were being told. But now I wonder, what if they had caught one of us off guard by ourselves some night? What if they'd had a crowbar? I'll admit, I had a crowbar in Korea. But it was primarily a conversation piece that hung on my wall locker, and I didn't carry it around. A lot of good it would've done me hanging in my room while I was facing a couple of armed giants out for revenge.

As for getting revenge yourself for certain matters, I'm not going to tell you what to do. But here's some advice from General Patton from *Patton's Principles* by Porter B. Williamson, and I think it's pretty good advice at that: "You go out of your way for revenge, and you will destroy yourself."

NOTES

1. Yeah, I remember the guy in *The Magnificent Seven* who beat the gunfighter with his switchblade, but that's Hollywood, folks.

2. If there was such a thing. By fair, I mean knowing he was coming and squaring up with the dude. Barehanded against a crowbar is definitely not fair, but no real fight is.

19

THE LAW

CHAPTER 3

"Better to keep peace than

to have to make peace."

—Anonymous

A major factor that comes into play before, during, and after physical confrontations is the law. Our society has made laws to protect the citizen from being preyed upon by those undesirable types who stalk so many of our streets looking for innocent victims. And we pay police officers to enforce those laws. Well, guess what? Hurting people is against the law! So if you are out there breaking bones and cracking skulls, be forewarned; you will probably end up talking to a police officer one of these days.

I'll tell you right up front, I'm on the side of the cops. You should at all times try to cooperate with any police officers you come in contact with. Hey, they have one hell of a tough job. Plus, they work in numbers quite often, and if you're in the wrong, you'll probably lose. I found out the hard way once when I was younger (and dumber) and got into it with an MP. I had a whole group of them on me real quick. They had me slammed up against a wall, all locked up, faster than I knew what was going on. I was in the MP station at the time and had just told the guys who were hauled in with me to be cool, so I guess you could really say that one was a lack of brain power on my part. So now I have grown up, and I have the utmost respect for *most* of our police officers. (There are a few bad apples in any group you look at.)

It's unfortunate that they can't be around at all times to protect people, but that's not their fault. So yes, we have to take care of ourselves at times. That's where awareness and, as a last resort, physical self-defense techniques come in. If you have a legitimate reason for hurting someone, then you won't have much to fear from the police and the legal system. (I know there are many who disagree with me here, but I try to make sure that I'm in the right and, consequently, don't have to worry about the law.)

All through this book I'll be saying how it's important to avoid the fight if possible. Not only will that save you from bodily harm, it will save you from trouble with the police. However, if you have tried to avoid the confrontation to no avail and have to resort to physical violence, it's important to have witnesses if possible. Sure, if you are jumped in a dark alley all by yourself you're not going to have any witnesses around. But many fights go down among other people, usually in bars. You want people to see and hear you try to avoid the conflict if possible. Just stating, "I don't want any trouble," or something to that effect, can do the job. You might want to alert the bouncer of the establishment that you feel trouble is going to start and you want to leave. Have him watch your back as you exit. There are many ways to establish that you didn't want any trouble.

One thing you don't ever want to do is let a bunch of people hear you talking about what you are going to do to someone. If you have to take someone out, fine. Don't talk about it. Especially if you threaten to kill someone. If you do kill him, even if it's unintentional, someone may remember you saying what you were going to do, and then you'll have to explain that you were just mouthing off and you didn't mean it. Hopefully they'll believe you and not start talking "premeditated" and all those other terms that will land you behind bars for a long time. So keep your mouth shut unless it serves a purpose.

Another good thing to have is friends that will back you no matter what. No, I'm not saying that you should have people lie for you. I'm just saying that it is good to have friends who will back you no matter what.

You see, just because you squash some guy and then boogie, it doesn't mean you aren't going to be talking to the cops later. My buddy Eric found this out one night in Korea. A loud-mouth was really acting up in a bar where Eric and a couple other snipers were playing pool. He was bad-mouthing the girls and everyone else in the place. When Eric told him to calm down, he started in on Eric. Eric tried to talk the guy down, but he'd have none of that. When he swung, Eric hit him. He didn't go down immediately, and he started to come at Eric again. So the next time Eric hit him with the pool cue he was holding. A few seconds after the guy hit the floor, Eric said 'bye and was on his way home—and he got there long before he could get caught by the MPs. (When Eric used to lead sniper school PT runs, the joke was that, instead of the double-time march that usually started the run, it was, "run like a deer—Go!")

The trouble was that there were people who knew who Eric was. So the next day Eric was called in by his commanding officer. It was standard procedure to give an Article 15 (nonjudicial punishment that could result in a loss of money, rank, or both along with extra duty and restriction to barracks) to anyone caught fighting. This would have hurt Eric's Special Forces packet he was planning to submit, so he chose to go through a court martial instead. (You can choose a court martial instead of any Article 15, but if you're found guilty, the punishment is a lot worse and it's considered a felony.)

So Eric went on trial. What saved him was the fact that there were others in the bar to testify that Eric had tried to get out of it without violence, and that the guy had swung at him first. So he was found not guilty and the case was dismissed. No blemishes on his record.

My dad's case was very similar when he wound up in court after breaking a guy's back. He and a friend had been jumped by a gang who got off by jumping GIs. Well, that night they jumped the wrong people, and my dad and his friend were sitting in a courtroom a while later on trial. This time it was some of the local people who testified to the fact that these guys went around beating up GIs. My dad was found not guilty on the grounds of self-defense. The only good thing about the whole ordeal is that it got my dad to thinking about what he was doing and what could happen.

Just like the military's standard procedure to give out Article 15s to soldiers caught fighting, many places have similar policies for civilians. There may be a set fine for all misdemeanor offenses. The time I smacked a guy for running into my parked truck it cost me $75. It was going to be $100, but I was able to talk the magistrate down. I can think of a lot better ways to spend $100 than just hitting a guy.

I probably could have left and not gotten caught, but I had to wait for the police to write up a report on my truck. It was actually me who called the cops. I never even thought that the guy would start crying about me hitting him. He wasn't hurt, just a sore jaw and a bloody mouth. But as it ended up, I received a misdemeanor assault citation and had to go see the magistrate the next week.

Actually, I was very lucky that night. It happened in a small town in Montana. In many places, I would have spent the night in the city jail. What if the guy I hit had smacked his head on the pavement when I knocked him down? I might have found out what the Montana State Prison was like, because I could have been facing manslaughter. You see, hitting someone because they messed with your things is not self-defense.

Anyway, as you can see, when it comes to physical confrontations you can very easily get into trouble, ranging from a hassle and some lost time to a jail sentence. (These are the things that happen when you *win* the fight, mind you.) So it really does pay to stay out of trouble. You do have the option of getting the hell out of Dodge, and at times it's a good option, before or after the shit goes down. I know I said that you should cooperate with the police, but I'll admit there have been many nights when I took off before the cops or MPs arrived. As I said earlier, they may find you the next day like they did with Eric. But then again, they may not. These are choices you will have to make on your own. I can't and shouldn't do it for you. I'm just giving you some things to think about.

So try and avoid physical confrontations, and if you can't, have some witnesses to testify that you tried to if you end up in the courtroom.

Peyton Quinn says he has an "I'm not going to prison" plan. Pretty good idea if you ask me. I've never been in prison, but I know enough about it that I don't want to go there. There are too many things here on the outside that I have fun doing. So, take Peyton's idea and create your own "stay out of prison" strategy.

AWARENESS

"A commander may be forgiven for being defeated, but never for being surprised."

—Old military maxim

I remember reading Animal's book *Cheap Shots, Ambushes, and Other Lessons* while in Korea. Right in the beginning he wrote, "Self-defense isn't fighting; it is awareness." Right, I thought. At least it showed me that this guy knew what he was talking about, and I kept reading to find out he knew a lot about quite a few of the things I was experiencing in the places I frequented.

There were a lot of things in that book I related to, but I was surprised that everyone didn't know some of it. It just seemed so obvious to me; doesn't everyone know that? Well, the answer is a big NO! I'm continually amazed at how many people walk through this world without knowing what is going on. Not only for self-defense purposes, but just for being able to enjoy life to the fullest. People miss so many things and then find themselves in undesirable circumstances that could have been avoided with a little awareness.

I remember a night in the dorms at the University of Montana. I worked both as night security and as a Resident Assistant while I was going to school. Both jobs require the person on duty to make rounds through the dorm. You just walk through every hour to make sure things are in order, and so on. One night I was making these rounds at about 2 a.m. I was on one of the female floors when I turned the corner of the hall and a girl exited the bathroom dressed in only a T-shirt. Nothing uncommon about that in a dorm, but the thing I didn't like was that she never even looked in my direction. So I was basically following her down the hall at two in the morning. She stopped at her door, and as she opened it I could have reached out and touched her; I had walked right up behind her. She went into the room never even knowing I was in the hall behind her.

That's scary! It's scary in the sense that she was so unaware of her surroundings. It would have taken less than a second to force her into the room after she had opened the door, and I'll let you imagine what could have happened next.

She was attractive, alone, undressed, and in a dimly lit hall at two in the morning. I stress that a person should be aware at all times, but especially in a situation like the one above. Anyone could have gotten into the dorm before we locked the doors at night. Or people can hang out outside and go in when a resident unlocks the door to enter or leave. Then they could hang around in TV rooms, the lounge, or the bathroom. Even though we tried to provide a safe environment, and they have increased the security measures since I left, it is still impossible to protect everyone at every given moment. (Our police forces have the same problem; that's why it is so important for people to look out for themselves, and being aware is the key to this.) All that would have been needed was for her to have looked both ways as she exited the bathroom. She would have seen me and recognized that I was the RA making rounds. No problem. If it had been a stranger, she could have said something like, "Are you looking for someone?" Whatever she might have done, at least she would have known that someone was in the hallway with her. With this knowledge, she wouldn't have been surprised as easily. Surprising victims is one of a criminal's advantages. If you take this element of surprise away, often a criminal will go look for an easier mark.

Often it is in places where we are most comfortable that we disregard the need to be aware. This is a mistake that has contributed to many undesirable events. The most obvious is when driving. We have all heard that the majority of accidents occur near the home. Why? Because the area is so familiar to people that they tend to not pay as close attention as they do to roads they have never driven on before. People get comfortable, then less aware, and finally careless. That's when accidents happen.

It's the same with awareness involving keeping yourself safe. We get careless doing simple things, and that's when we hurt ourselves. I've never fallen from a cliff, because I don't like heights so much and I'm damn careful up there. (Jumping from a plane is another thing; heights aren't so bad when you have a parachute on. Airborne!) But I have fallen doing simple stuff. The thing is, we need to be aware at these times also. People get assaulted and raped in their homes. The 83-year-old lady I mentioned earlier in this book was raped at her own house in the middle of the afternoon. In Helena, Montana, no less—an area that isn't known for violent crime. Sometimes I think it is only lower because not many people live here. As more and more people move in, the crime seems to increase. In the chapter on women, I talk about when I had my wallet stolen by a group of kids in Ho Chi Minh City (Saigon) when I was on a trip to Vietnam. I wasn't being aware of what was going on. I got careless. It happens to everyone; it's just that sometimes the consequences are much more severe for some people than others.

So even though there have been times when I wasn't as aware as I should have been, let's look at a time when I did things right. I had just gotten off a bus in Bangkok, Thailand. It was an all-night bus from Chang Mai, and it arrived at Kao San Road at 5 a.m. So there I was, alone, tired, with my backpack and a waist pouch that held my camera, money, passport, and so on, and nowhere to go. Things weren't open yet. A cab driver stopped and wanted to know if I wanted to go to the airport. I told him I was just waiting for a place to open to get breakfast and then a room. I planned on staying in Bangkok for a couple of days before heading south to Samet Island.

I was walking down a deserted street just off Kao San Road when I noticed two guys following me. No big deal at this point; they were just going in the same direction, right? I decided to turn around and go in the other direction anyway. I didn't want to travel too far with all my stuff, and I wanted to get into a place to eat as soon as one opened. I was hungry. I acknowledged them as I passed. At this point I wasn't even thinking anything, but I was aware that they were there.

I went back to Kao San Road and sat down on some steps in front of a closed-up shop. The place I wanted to eat breakfast was located just across the street. I had my bag sitting beside me, and I was just waiting for the sun to come up and for the area to come alive. (Kao San Road is very alive at times.) Lo and behold, here come the two bozos again. I call them bozos because they were so obvious. They could have worn signs on their chests that said, "I'm looking to rob someone." They had circled around a couple of blocks and were coming down the street in a different direction from where I had just seen them. I recognized them, though, and watched them out of the corner of my eye as they meandered up the street toward me. They arrived at the steps I was sitting on, and instead of passing, they went up the steps behind me and pretended to be looking into the closed shop.

Now, come on, was this an "interview" or what? A criminal interview is when a criminal has the intent to commit a crime and is sizing up his victim. The interview is the process of looking for the lack of awareness in the potential victim and the positioning for the crime.[1]

Anyway, I felt it was very obvious, and it is if you are aware. I actually chuckled to myself and thought, "This is just like the situations Animal talks about in his lectures." Then I had to decide what I wanted to do about it. I knew for damn sure I wasn't going to let these two get away with my stuff. It wasn't worth a whole hell of a lot, but I wasn't going to let it go nonetheless.

The two weren't Thai; I believe they were from the Middle East somewhere, but I'm not sure. They weren't that big, and I wasn't really concerned with their doing me any physical harm. In other words, with my sometimes cocky attitude, I was pretty sure I could handle myself against them. There were only two other considerations. First, they might have been armed. I didn't see any weapons yet, but one or both of them might have had a small knife. Then there was my bag. If one of them tied me up for just a second, the other could get away with my stuff, and wasn't that what I didn't want to happen? I'm sure they knew the area much better than I did, so it was doubtful I'd catch them if they disappeared in the alleys.

I stood up immediately when they moved behind me, and I thought of a couple of possible alternatives: I could just confront them (once they knew I was onto them they might just leave), or I could start walking down the street, and when they followed, I'd be the one in charge. (What sniper can't ditch a couple of goons?) But then the perfect opportunity appeared. The restaurant I was waiting for opened its gate. So I picked up my bag and started to walk across the street to see when they would start serving.

An interesting thing happened then. A cab pulled up and the driver motioned me over to him. I was about to wave him off when I recognized that it was the same cabby I had been talking to earlier. I went over to his cab, with my bags in hand, to see what he wanted. "Those are very bad men," he said. "You should not be here."

"I know," I replied. "I was just leaving."

"Good," he said and drove away as I headed across the street. This just reinforced my opinion that even though there are a lot of scum out there, there are also decent people throughout the world. There is a Thai cab driver who took the time to warn a tourist of possible trouble, even when he knew I wouldn't be a fare.

This didn't end it, though. I wasn't letting on that I knew what these two were up to, but you would think that they might figure it out. They didn't. I sat down in the restaurant at a table in the rear next to the wall. I was facing forward so I could see outside into the street. The place didn't have a front door; the whole front was open. A big gate was lowered at night, like the shops in most malls. After I ordered, I noticed that only one of the two men was still standing on the steps. A few minutes later, the second guy came in and sat at the front corner table of the place I was in. Funny thing—he didn't order anything when the waiter went up to him. He was facing outside also, keeping an eye on his buddy across the street.

I finished my meal and the two were still in position. It was still dark, but I knew it would be light in another 20 or 30 minutes and that the street would come alive at that time and I could go find a room in a cheap guest house and dump my belongings. So, should I go outside and see what the two would do? Hell no. Why even bother and take the chance? If I hadn't had my big bag I would have, but I didn't want to lose my clean clothes. So I pulled out my *Lonely Planet* guidebook and started to read up on a couple of places I wanted to visit. The sun came up, people showed up, and the two gave up.

Because of my awareness and knowing how to recognize and avoid dangerous situations, I didn't have any problems that morning. I didn't get hurt, and I didn't lose any of my stuff. Anyone could have done the same thing. The sad truth is that many people fall prey to these types of predators when a little awareness and avoidance is all that is needed to ensure one's safety. The only thing this didn't do is satisfy the urge I had to smash the two for even thinking about ripping me off. But that's the part of me I've learned to control. So I don't do those things when there are nonviolent alternatives. Violence is the first option and the last choice of the competent.

Many people confuse self-defense with the ability to fight or beat someone up. This concept is further enhanced by "self-defense courses" that teach martial art techniques only. I don't particularly agree with this concept. If you look at the term self-defense, where does hurting someone else come in? Self-defense is for keeping yourself from being hurt. That's the ultimate goal, to ensure your own safety. The number-one way to ensure that you will not be physically harmed is to avoid engaging in any physical altercation. You can do this by being aware. I won't say that you can avoid 100 percent of the things that may happen. I talk in another chapter about how you may decide to engage in a physical confrontation for one reason or another. I do believe that you have to fight at times.

This choice is yours. However, avoidance is still the best alternative and could be used in many more situations if people would just wake up and pay attention to what's going on around them.

This concept of not fighting was shown well in one scene of *Enter the Dragon*. Sure the movie had enormous amounts of fighting, but that's how you get people to watch martial art movies. There was the scene, though, where Bruce Lee and the others were on the boat that was taking them to the island where the big tournament was being held. A minor character who had been bullying some of the others on the boat asked Bruce what style he practiced. "The art of fighting without fighting," the hero answered. When the aggressor pressed him to show this art, Bruce told him that they should take a smaller boat, which was connected to the larger vessel with a rope, to the nearby shore where they would have more room. He let the bully climb into the smaller boat, and then he threatened to release the rope and set the bully adrift if he tried to get back into the larger boat. This trick brought laughs and cheers from the others aboard the ship. This is exactly what I'm talking about. Violence is the last choice of the competent. Bruce Lee won the confrontation without throwing a single blow.

In real life, Animal says the same thing. We were talking one night, and he was telling me how he likes to send drunks down the street when he's working a place as a bouncer or cooler. He likes sending them down to City Hall to complain that the bar won't serve them any more because of the law concerning serving intoxicated persons. Who knows how many find City Hall, or wait till it opens. (That would be pretty amusing, though, wouldn't it?) But the problem is out of the bar, and that's what concerns Marc. He states, "I figure if I have to throw a punch or get physical, I've messed up somewhere. I should be able to recognize situations and defuse them before that." It sure isn't because Marc doesn't know how to get physical, it's just that he's a professional and he knows better ways to solve problems.

Actually, I think Animal may be just a little lazy. He's figured out what most people who work as bouncers, coolers, concert security, and the like figure out: it's much easier to stop problems before punches start flying. It seems like quite often when you pull someone off of someone else while you're breaking fights up, they swing at you. I actually had a guy hit me once and then apologize. I was breaking the fight up and he clipped me in the jaw with an elbow—not bad, but it smarted. He saw who I was and stopped, "I'm sorry man. I didn't know it was you." Yes, stopping things before they get started is much easier—nothing gets broken, no police get involved, and no one gets hurt. (Getting popped in the mouth and having your lip all swelled up really sucks when you want to kiss someone.) The same thing goes for the street. It's a lot easier to recognize and avoid trouble than it is to get yourself out of it once it's begun.

I'm not advocating that you live your life in paranoia. Don't go around jumping at every loud noise and being afraid of your own shadow. But you should be aware of what's going on. Often the levels of awareness are ranked. They may be labeled as numbers or colors or any other way you want to label them, but I'll use the colors that are commonly used in the military. You have four levels: white, yellow, orange, and red.

The first level is white. This is when you don't have any awareness at all. It is the state where you are not ready for anything. The girl I wrote about in the dorm was at this level, as are most people as they go about their daily activities in life. In this state, people are oblivious to their surroundings and the things that are happening around them. Not only are you an easy victim when you live in this state, but you miss so much around you that you might otherwise enjoy.

Unfortunately, many people drive automobiles in this state of unawareness. They will drive along never noticing the potential dangers that could easily be recognized and avoided if they would just wake up and pay attention. I come from Montana, where a lot of deer are killed on the highway each year. Some are killed because a person is driving faster than the visibility permits. That happened to me one year. I saw them, but I was going too fast to stop in time. I don't drive like that at night anymore. But many of the deer are killed because the driver isn't paying attention; in fact, that's the cause of most accidents. When driving, and preferably most of the time, I recommend that a person stay in level yellow.

Yellow is the second level of awareness. This is a state where you have a heightened sense of what's going on around you. Don't mistake this for paranoia. I just recommend that you acknowledge what is going on in your surroundings. Naturally, there are times when you need to be a little more alert than others, but by keeping your head up and your eyes open you will be able to recognize many possible hostile situations and raise your state of awareness to orange as the situation dictates.

Orange is the third state of awareness, and it is entered when you realize that something is going down that may be detrimental to your well-being. Often it is only a feeling, and many will shift into this mode automatically. A little comment to a buddy, such as, "Shit's going down over there," or "Heads up, trouble's coming" will often alert friends to go to orange also. When you go to orange, you realize that some form of action is needed. It's time to avoid or confront. You need to make some decisions, and you need to make them quickly.

The last level is red. That's when you are out of the frying pan and into the fire. When you decide that you have no choice but to fight, you move to red and you give it all you have. Hit hard and decisively—your goal is to end it quickly to ensure your safety.

This labeling is just an easy way to show how you can have different levels of readiness or alertness. At certain times one is more appropriate than the others. Practice staying at the second level, yellow, and you will be able to recognize many more threats in time to do something about them. You will also get lost less, find things more quickly, and generally be more informed about things. (Because when you pay more attention, you see and learn more.)

Here is a fun drill you can do at your leisure, and it will increase your level of awareness and help your reaction time when you get into trouble. My dad taught it to me a long time ago when I was learning to drive. As I was driving, he would have me think of what I'd do and where I'd go if something happened at that moment. (It's a lot better to go into a ditch instead of colliding into another vehicle in a head-on.) So you play a game and think of what you would do. He would also take me out on icy roads and have me slam on the brakes to see what it was like and learn how to handle an out-of-control vehicle. His teaching included making me stop on ice with the brakes and by shifting to lower gears. (It's amazing that so many people in the southern states don't receive any of this training, and when they get out on icy roads there are accidents galore.)

Now expand this game to other areas. Look for places a mugger or attacker could hide. Think of what you would do if something happened right now. What would you do? Where would you go? Where are you? If you had to make an emergency call on a corner pay phone, would you know where you're at? Many people don't. "I'm, uh, by this bar, uh, well, I think it's on, uh, you know where the big factory is?" And they go on like this when precious seconds count in so many emergencies. So start paying more attention to your surroundings and make a special effort to be more alert and notice things on a regular basis. Eventually you'll be more aware when you aren't thinking about it.

It's not only great to know what's going on around you, it's essential. However, this is only part of being aware. You must also be aware of how you are affecting the things that are going on. Let's go back to the ice. It isn't enough to know that you are driving on a slick road. You must know what the consequences of your actions will be. You need to know how the speed you're driving will affect things as well as knowing how you'll affect things by slamming on the brakes or shifting to a lower gear.

I can go into a biker bar and get along fine, or I can go in and get creamed—I mean really stomped—and it all depends on how I act. Sure I know what kind of place I'm in. I'm aware, but I need to also be aware of what I'm doing to affect the situation. Going in bad-mouthing bikers and complaining about someone's Harley isn't very conducive to one's overall health.

So be alert and pay attention to your surroundings, but also be aware of how your interaction with the situation affects what's going on. These simple rules will enable you to recognize and avoid most hostile situations, and they will aid you in coming out the victor when you decide that you need to engage in a violent encounter, or when there is no other alternative than a physical confrontation.

NOTES

1.   For a more detailed description of the process and the different types of interviews, read *Safe in the City*, by Marc "Animal" MacYoung and Chris Pfouts. Or view Marc's video *Safe in the Street*. You may also want to check out a crime avoidance lecture.

GETTING PHYSICAL

PART TWO

"A warrior is someone who is always striving for self-mastery, to improve himself and to better serve his goals."

—Richard Strozzi Heckler

In Search of the Warrior Spirit

The reality of fighting is that you have to get physical unless you use Bruce Lee's "fighting without fighting" technique that I mentioned while discussing awareness. By the way, Sun Tzu said, "To win without fighting is best" in *The Art of War* 2,000 years ago.

There are many physical skills, but some are more important than others when it comes to fighting. You need to have balance and mobility to be able to use the tools at your disposal—tools like your hands, feet, elbows, knees, and other body parts that can dish out damage to your opponent. You need to be able to fight from different ranges, including the ground.

To become proficient in the physical aspects needed for fighting, you need to train, and train realistically. Chris Caracci has a saying: "Train as you live. Live as you train." And no matter what you know, you will be better equipped to handle any situation if you are fit. A sound program of anaerobic and aerobic exercise will ensure this.

BALANCE, STANCE, AND FOOTWORK

CHAPTER 5

"Careful is a naked man

climbin' a bobwire fence."

—Ken Alstad

Savvy Sayin's

In order to do any of the physical techniques you learn effectively, you have to have good balance. Balance is required for a proper stance and for movement during the encounter. So let's look at each of these related areas.

BALANCE AND MOBILITY

I'm going to talk a little about both of these because they are so closely related. Sure, you can be mobile without having much balance, but you'll more than likely end up on your ass. And if you have great

41

balance in a stance but can't move, you're not going to fare well either. Fighting requires a combination of the two. If you can move and stay in balance while doing it, you'll have a great advantage in most physical altercations. (It helps a lot when you're walking across an icy parking lot wearing cowboy boots too.)

Actually, balance and mobility are two of the most critical aspects in fighting or combat. Everything you do will be centered on being able to move without losing your footing or balance. If you possess both, you can be in control of the confrontation; if not, you will be hanging in the breeze when you don't want to be.

Real fights happen blindingly fast, and you have to be able to move lightning quick. An unbalanced fighter will not be able to react as fast as the guy who's in control. This is especially true when something goes wrong, and believe me, sooner or later something will go astray. You'll throw that never-fail technique, and all of a sudden your opponent won't be where he's supposed to be. If you don't react quickly and counter his counter, you're going down. Keeping your balance is critical to being able to change directions mid swing. Once you've overextended yourself, the options you have are greatly reduced. When you have proper balance, you can move in any direction.

STANCE

There is a lot written about and taught in the way of proper stance. In the classical martial arts there are numerous stances for different applications. Most of these are used in katas and forms and are not really practical on the street. When it comes down to it, you probably won't have time to get into a "proper" stance anyway. You aren't going to have a referee starting the confrontation, giving you the time to "get into your stance." The stance you start fighting from will be whatever position you are in when the fight breaks out. You may not be standing at all, but sitting on a stool or chair. (You think people don't get hit while sitting down? I'll tell you different.)

Even though this may happen, it is good to get into a fighting stance, or a position to act from as soon as possible. (You will have to initially act from whatever position you are in, but you'll naturally fall into your preferred fighting stance as you are reacting.) And you will need a stance to train from during your sparring matches. A building is only as strong as its foundation, and the stance while fighting is the foundation to develop strong balance and footwork. Once you have become comfortable moving while training, you will instinctively be able to move in an actual confrontation.

There are two main schools of thought on stances. One believes in leading with your strong hand. This means if you are right-handed, your right foot and right hand will be in front. The other widely practiced method is rooted in boxing, where you lead with your weak hand. This is illustrated by a boxer snaking out lightning-quick jabs with his lead hand to set his opponent up for the big right cross, the power punch. Which is better? It just depends on your personal preference and training. I recommend that you become comfortable using both. Learn to lead with either side. When I spar, I will often switch my lead. Sometimes I will stay in the classic boxing stance, and at other times I lead with my right. Mix it up and see what works best for you individually.

No matter what stance you choose, there are some basic considerations you need to think about and incorporate. These are aspects that any good stance will provide.

First, you should be able to move. The stance you choose should provide the mobility to move in all directions. You should be able to close and attack as well as retreat. It is necessary to be able to move to the sides, for this will enable you to move off center line, which is important in defending yourself. You should also be able to pivot 180 degrees. Many defensive and offensive moves rely on the ability to pivot. If your stance is too wide, you will be slowed down, and if your feet are too close together, you'll lose your balance easily. Find a comfortable stance in the middle that allows you to move quickly in each direction while maintaining your balance.

Next, you should be able to protect your lower extremities while in your stance. The stance should give you the ability to protect both your knees and your groin. Moving out of the way of a knee kick or rolling with it to prevent injury should be possible from your stance. Some of the classical rigid stances leave the knees open for damaging kicks. Protecting them is extremely important. I don't have to tell many men that protecting the family jewels is also an important consideration. Pivoting away or pinching off incoming groin kicks should be possible from a proper stance.

I personally like to be on the balls of my feet. This was drilled into me by my father when I was younger and practicing basketball. "Get up on the balls of your feet so you can move faster," he would yell when I'd be out practicing flat-footed.

Remember *Rocky III*? Rocky finally learned how to box under the tutelage and guidance of Apollo Creed. Apollo had him up on the balls of his feet working on his footwork. Later the sports commentator was surprised at the fleet-footed challenger, no longer the flat-footed brawler Rocky had been. This was just a movie, but boxers generally do have good footwork. Actually, boxers usually do pretty well in the street. I believe that much of this is due to the excellent physical condition most boxers stay in, as well as the actual full-contact training they go through. Boxing toughens a person up and conditions him to absorb physical punishment. My good friend Jeff was a college boxer before he entered the army, and he definitely knew how to apply those skills on the street and in the bars. He was a southpaw (lefty) to boot, and that can be advantageous also.

Some people advocate staying more flat-footed. This is okay and may be more suitable for some people. You will be a little slower, but you may be more solid. You may have an easier time keeping your balance and staying stable with your feet flat on the ground. It's also not as tiring as staying on your toes. That's why boxers aren't dancing around as much in the later rounds and are more flat-footed then. They're worn out. This really isn't as much of a concern in street fights, since they don't usually last that long.

I personally think you should do some training on the balls of your feet, as it will help you no matter which way you choose in an actual fight. Get to know the strengths and weaknesses of both alternatives.

Whether you stay flat-footed or get up on the balls of your feet, you need to keep your knees bent. This is crucial to keeping your balance. If you have ever skied or skated, you know how important it is to bend your knees. Try going down the slopes with your legs straight sometime. Knees bent and proper placement of your feet—not too narrow and not too wide—will give you that foundation of balance and mobility. This, in turn, will enable you to achieve power and leverage.

The last thing I'll mention about a proper stance is the position of the hands. Like everything else, there are many schools of thought on this aspect too. The most important thing is to have your hands in a position where they can protect your upper body. Don't hold them too stiff. You should have them relaxed in order to move faster.

Some people teach clenching your fists lightly, and some people prefer to leave their hands open. Just don't clench your fists tight. This will tense the arm and hamper quickness, besides increasing fatigue. I personally will do both, depending on the situation and what I'm doing. Sometimes I will have them lightly clenched, and at other times I keep them open and slightly cupped. I think there are more things you can do with the open hand, so I keep them open more than not.

It's not just your hands that will defend you. Keep your elbows in a position that offers you some protection. Watch a boxer cover up; he'll take blows all along the arm rather than getting hit in a more vital spot like the head or body. After a long time, those arm shots will wear a fighter's arms down. But in the fast and furious bar brawl, you'll take the blow on the arm and then deliver one to your opponent's head and end the fight, right? Protect yourself; it's important.

FOOTWORK

Proper basic footwork will enable you to move quickly and efficiently while attacking and defending. You won't be dancing around like a professional boxer, but moving in quick while keeping your balance to get the job done, and then moving out just as fast. Remember that the quicker you end the fight the better.

There are three basic purposes of footwork. One is to move in on your opponent. The next is to move away from your opponent. And the last is to set your opponent up. Anything else is just a variation of one of these.

There are four basic directions you can go: forward, backward, to the left, and to the right. Then you have diagonals that are just variations or combinations of these. To have effective footwork, basically you need to follow this formula: when moving forward, the front foot moves first; when moving backward, the rear foot moves first; when moving to the left, the left foot moves first; and when moving to the right, the right foot moves first.

I like to emphasize stepping and sliding. Step with your lead foot and then slide the other foot. This can be done very quickly and will aid you in remaining balanced and centered. Keep the distances moved symmetrical. In other words, if you step forward eight inches with your lead foot, slide your rear foot forward the same distance, eight inches. You want to keep the feet a consistent length apart.

The step can be quickened by springing off the opposite foot. So if you are moving forward, you spring off the rear foot when you initiate the step and then the rear foot slides up. If you are retreating, you spring off your front foot as you step back with your rear foot. Then you slide the front foot back.

Practice moving around like this until you can move about gracefully. You want to be able to attain the smoothest and most coordinated movement between your feet. This will only come with practice.[1]

A very good activity to increase your mobility skills is dancing. My dad used to always tell me I should learn different dances and dance more. It develops balance, coordination, agility, and footwork. I didn't listen too well and am not a very good dancer yet, but I'm learning some now. When Marc MacYoung asked me if I danced, I told him not much, but that my dad had always told me I should. Animal's reply was, "You should have listened to him." Besides helping with your footwork, it's a great way to meet women. My buddy Dave is an excellent dancer, and he never has any trouble finding someone to jitterbug with. All the women want to get out there and be twisted, spun, and flipped by him, and often he's the star of the dance floor when we go out. Dancing hurts a lot less than fighting, not to mention it doesn't get you in near the trouble. Wouldn't you rather go home with some cutie after a night of dancing instead of going home with a broken nose after a night of fisticuffs?

Ranges

I want to discuss a little about the ranges of fighting. It's your footwork that will get you in and out of these ranges, so I'm including them in this chapter.

There are basically four ranges that all fights fall into. You have long range, or kicking range; medium range, or punching range; trapping range, or infighting; and you have your wrestling range, or grappling on the ground. Every fight will fall under one or more of these ranges before it's through. Often the fight will fall into all of them before it's over.

Each of these ranges has its strengths and weaknesses, advantages and disadvantages, and different techniques and defenses. It's a personal choice as to which of these ranges you prefer to fight in. Different body types and styles lend themselves to different ranges. You should, however, understand the different ranges and how a person will operate from each.

A long-range fighter will try and keep his opponent away from him, relying on strong kicks as his primary weapons. Tae kwon do is a long-range fighting system. It works best in an open area with a lot of space to move around. Usually this type of fighting is suited to the taller, long-limbed individual. A medium-range fighter relies on strong punching techniques. A boxer is an example of a medium-range fighter. An infighter, or someone who likes to fight at an extremely close range, likes to use techniques such as headbutts, elbow strikes, and knee strikes. This kind of fighter does extremely well in tight situations. Often this style of fighting is used by shorter individuals, as is the next range. The last range is on the ground. This is the range a wrestler or jujutsu practitioner will excel in. If you have seen any of the Gracies take a guy to the floor, you know how effective their art is in this range. It involves all sorts of wrestling and grappling techniques, including chokes and submission holds.

It should be fairly obvious that each of the styles that excels in one range will fall short in another. Someone who relies on kicks will be in trouble in tight quarters with a wrestler who takes him down. On the other hand, in an open parking lot where the tae kwon do man can keep the wrestler away until he lands that devastating kick, the encounter may end up differently. All styles and ranges have their pluses and minuses. You always want to try and control the range you fight from to give yourself the advantage, but sometimes this is rather difficult. You may end up in a situation where you aren't the one controlling the range. (Wouldn't it be nice if you could always pick the who, when, where, why, and all the other variables?) Since you can't, it's important that you know how to function outside of your preferred distance. This means train in all of them.

Sometimes it's wise to change distance if the other guy's preferred style is the same as yours. If you can fight from a different range, you may have a better advantage over him after switching. I personally like infighting and liked to slam dudes into the wall, where I could then use my knees and elbows to my best advantage. But against another infighter, I'd rather stay farther outside and use a good kick to the knee and some hand strikes before going inside. It just depends on the opponent's level of ability in each range.

When you're practicing, be sure to include practice for all four ranges. You'll have your preferred range and style, but supplement it with training in the others. The complete fighter can fight from any range, and that should be your goal in training. In the parking lot, in the alley, and on the floor, wherever you end up, you want to be able to handle the situation. Control the range if you can, but never let the range control you.

NOTES

1. After you get these basics mastered, you can start working with more advanced types of footwork like crossover steps and other movements that involve crossing the feet. These are worth knowing, but I won't go into them here.

DEFENSE

CHAPTER 6

"Don't get hit!—defense simplified."

—Anonymous

There have been a lot of things written and said about defense, but when it comes down to it, the primary objective is to avoid being hurt by your opponent. The best way to achieve this is to not let him hit you, or at least to lessen the force of the blows that do land. You should also be putting yourself in a position to counter with your own strikes, or to escape, whichever suits the situation.

Many people still believe that the best defense is a good offense. General Patton said it best when he told his troops, "Don't worry about your flanks. Let the enemy worry about his flanks." This may be true in the case of war, but I'm hoping you are paying attention to the things I'm writing and aren't going out on the offensive. If this is the case, you will need to know some defensive moves in order to thwart your attacker's first onslaught and then return fire with your offensive techniques. At this time, yes, give it all you have and get it over with. The longer it lasts, the more of a chance you may get hurt. But you're going to need to defend before you go on the offense.

GET OUT OF THE WAY

Often, one of the simplest defensive moves is getting out of the way. I read a quip in a newspaper a while back claiming that every hostile male animal signals a charge by lowering his head. It listed examples of elephants, bulls, and human boxers. Quite often, the untrained bar fighter will lower his head and charge also. A simple step to the side can get you out of the way and put you in a position to send him to the floor. This is why footwork and balance are so important. They enable you to move.

You also want to be good at backpedaling. This can be very effective against a charge also. Say the opponent's a football player and he's coming in head down for a tackle. As you backpedal, grab the back of his head and drive it toward your feet. He kisses the pavement and you are left standing. Too many people just meet the charge head-on and both go down to the floor. Never meet someone's force head-on if you can redirect it. You can always throw a chair or something in his way as you backpedal out of there.

BLOCKS AND PARRIES

Blocks are the basic defensive techniques taught in most martial arts. The hard karate styles and tae kwon do use very rigid blocks with names like high block, low block, and so on.

I learned these blocks and performed them while doing katas, but I can't recall ever using one in a real fight. I do think that the practicing of them helps develop overall hand-eye coordination, and that they may aid you in throwing some sloppy form of block in a real encounter. I said I never used any of the blocks I practiced; that doesn't mean I didn't stop some punch with some hybrid what-do-you-call-that-kind-of-block to save my head from getting creamed at times. None of the fights I've been in or witnessed looked like the katas we used to practice, but I think I'd be pretty ignorant to say katas are completely worthless. I do feel that they have value, and if you are in a school that uses katas in practice, give them 110 percent. You will fight as you train.

The thing I don't care for with a lot of these blocks is that they rely on force stopping force. Not that they don't work in some situations; it's just that I would rather use a parry or open-hand slapping block in most cases. A parry is technically different from a block in that it is used to redirect an assailant's blow rather than stop it like most traditional hard blocks.

With most parries, you will redirect the blow to the outside, inside, or downward. You will do this with an open hand, and you will find that they are a lot quicker than many of the traditional blocks.

With this said, I still believe that you should learn and practice a variety of blocks and parries during your training. After all, this is what's going to keep you from getting hurt in a confrontation. There are so many different blocks and parries out there that I'm not going to go into them here. It's true that for every offensive technique, there's a defensive technique or counter. So learn them well.

One key that you should include with your training in blocks and parries is movement. Learn to block while moving—forward, to the sides, and backward. Rarely in a real fight are you both going to be immobile. Many times a block or parry that wouldn't work standing still will be all you need if you are moving out of the way at the same time. One of my favorites is to step to my left to avoid an overhand right, while using an open-hand parry with my right hand to direct his arm past me. Then I'm in a position to do all sorts of neat things.

SLIPPING

Slipping is a term that means just avoiding your opponent's punch or kick without moving out of range. Bobbing and weaving in boxing is a method of slipping an opponent's punch. A miss is a miss. When I was in Korea I became used to the cabs, trucks, and other vehicles on the road just missing me as I walked down the narrow streets. It got to where a miss was a miss. What's the difference if the truck was 10 feet away or 2 inches, just as long as the mirror didn't clip you. A punch or a kick is the same thing. It only needs to miss you by a fraction of an inch to lose its effectiveness. You slip a blow by leaning sideways, backward, or forward under the incoming strike. Apollo taught this to Rocky in *Rocky III*, and he used it quite effectively in the end fight. He was slipping and ducking Clubber's blows and then went on to launch his own attack.

Many times this is one of the best ways to avoid being hit, because it often leaves you in a good position to counter. My buddy John was excellent at ducking an overhand right. It was his favorite move, and he knew how to read an opponent to know when it would work. As he ducked and slipped the punch, he would send a right into the guy's solar plexus and then come up with a left hook to the jaw. It was a great combination and one that he practiced and used regularly.

TAKING A PUNCH

Hopefully, if you block, parry, slip, dodge, and get out of the way, you won't have to take many punches. But the fact is, if you fight, you're going to get hit. This doesn't mean the end of the world; there are some measures you can use to lessen the impact of the blow and keep on going.

The number-one deciding factor of how a blow is going to affect you is your mental state. If you are prepared to take a blow and have trained with some full-contact sparring, you know what a punch feels like. You don't want to experience your first hit on the street. It actually scares many people, so accepting the fact that you will be hit and going through it first in training will eliminate this fear. (If not completely, at least it will lessen it so that you won't be immobilized after first contact.)

When you get hit, follow the path of least resistance. Relax and flow or roll with the punch. When you are relaxed, your body is more resilient and less prone to serious injury. For example, if a right cross connects with your jaw, it will be more than likely on your left side. As the blow connects, you want to be turning your head to the right, or rolling with the punch. At the same time, you can rotate your body in the direction of the punch to lessen its effect. Bend your knees. You can absorb some of the blow through bending the knees.

If it's a body blow, you should exhale forcefully. This will keep you from getting the air knocked out of you. Some people like to yell when doing this. A yell can startle your opponent and give you the motivation to launch your counter. You can also shed blows to the body. You do this by pivoting and turning your body. Imagine a pole running down through the top of your head to the ground. Rotate on this center axis. As your body turns, the blow slides off.[1] Getting hit isn't the end of the fight, so train to take a punch and then practice your defense so you won't have to.

Don't let the length of this chapter lead you to believe defense isn't important. After awareness, it's probably the most important thing that will keep you from being injured on the street. You should spend a considerable amount of time training in defensive moves and counters. These are what will save you in an ambush.

I'll leave you with a couple of words of wisdom Animal gave me in the gym. He recognized that I'm better at protecting my head than my body. This is primarily due to the fact that I've always been in good shape and didn't mind absorbing body blows. Like Animal said, "You're getting older now, and you don't want to put your body through punishment it doesn't have to take." The point is, you should protect everything. It's kind of like the guy who turns 100 and says, "If I'd known I was going to live so long, I would have taken better care of myself." Protect and take care of your body; it's the only one you have. And if you don't, where else are you going to live?

NOTES

1. Marc MacYoung shows this concept well in his knife fighting videos. Not only will the pivot help you shed blows, it can get you completely out of the way also. The simple move has a variety of uses.

USING YOUR HANDS

CHAPTER 7

"Feint east, strike west."

—author unknown

Thirty-Six Strategies

We use our hands for just about everything, and they are a pretty versatile tool for all kinds of tasks. Fighting is no exception. I think that because we are so used to using our hands, it is easier to learn hand techniques than those with the feet. (Not to mention the whole balance thing.)

PUNCHING

There are a lot of opinions about punching and striking with the hands. I, myself, have conflicting views and opinions at times. I know that punching a guy in the

57

mouth with your knuckles hurts. I have a nice little scar to prove it. (Teeth are hard and they cut.) People break their hands punching things all the time. Even professional boxers and full-contact karate men break their hands wearing wraps and gloves. I heard Don "The Dragon" Wilson, the full-contact fighter turned actor, say that he's broken his hands 10 times with gloves on. Even so, I think it is important to be proficient at the basic punches. Good old Western boxing teaches the basic three: the jab, the cross, and the hook. So let's look at these first. Right after we look at the basics of making a fist.

To make a fist, curl up your fingers tight. You want your hand and arm relaxed right up to the moment of impact. Then you want your fist tight. Keep your thumb on the outside of the fist or you're going to break it. Yeah, I know this is basic, but some people still do it wrong. When you deliver the blow, strike with the portion of the fingers just below the knuckles. The first two knuckles should be the ones you use. I don't like those strikes with extended knuckles. I like a good tight fist with none of that sticking-a-knuckle-out crap. So now let's use that fist.

The basic jab or straight jab is primarily used to set your opponent up or to stun and distract him. It is the least power-ful, but it is the quickest. It is performed by shooting your lead fist straight out to your target. Remember that the shortest distance from point A to point B is usually a straight line. (I say usually because I've been in the field when a straight line on the map included going over a mother of a mountain. It was much shorter and easier to go around the thing.) Anyway, in this case with the jab, you want to go in a straight line.

To deliver the quickest blow, shoot the jab out straight to where you want it to connect. Then bring it back as fast as you shot it out there. This is important with all punches. You want the punch to go in as fast as possible, of course, but you need to retract your arm as quickly as possible also. Otherwise you can have a whole slew of nasty things done to it while it's hanging out there—things that go snap, crackle, and pop.

Another tip for all punching is to never fully extend your arm and lock it out. Always keep a little bend in it. One, it will aid in that quick retraction. Two, if you don't get it out in time, a straight locked-out arm is much easier to do all those cracking, popping, and snapping things to. You do not want this to happen, so don't lock out your arm.

The cross, or overhand cross, is the next punch we'll look at. This is your basic punch coming from your rear hand. Most right-handed boxers lead with their left so that their strongest hand is ready to deliver the more powerful blow, the cross. It's slower because it's going a farther distance. But you can put your weight into it and knock a guy's head off.

You develop the power for this blow with footwork and by using your body. Don't overextend yourself and have that arm hanging in the breeze with your balance all shot to hell. Remember to keep your other hand up for defense when throwing any punch. Keep your guard up! If your opponent slips the punch, you can bet he's sending something your way. And you don't want it.

The last basic boxing punch is the hook. This can be a powerful blow if you get the pivot right. You turn with the foot, knee, and hip as you deliver the blow. Your arm makes a circular motion around the guy's hands to connect with his head or body if you're throwing a low hook. Don't just use your arm. The power comes from the whole body. Again, remember to keep your chin down and your other hand up.

If you haven't learned these basics, do. Get someone who knows how to execute them to show you. Then practice, practice, practice. Practice putting these punches into effective combinations. Practice your footwork with these punches, closing the distance, getting back out, and so on. Say what you will about boxing, but I've seen boxers tear the hell out of other fighters. My buddy Jeff was a college boxer before he went Airborne, and that stuff came in handy on the street. It's not surprising that most PKA (Professional Karate Association) and other karate matches look like boxing bouts instead of dojo sparring sessions.

The Hammer Fist

Find a brick wall and hit it with a normal fist with your knuckles as hard as you feel comfortable with. (Don't break your hand or anything just to prove a point.) Then hit the same wall with a fist, but use the meaty portion of your hand as the striking surface (The same surface as if you were pounding on a table, hence the name hammer fist). Which hurts less? You can deliver a much more powerful blow without injuring your hand by using the bottom of your fist. This is why the hammer fist was one of my favorite ways to strike someone.

If you are facing a skilled fighter, you're not going to throw this punch. If you do, he's going to do a couple of things. First, he'll set his alarm clock and take a nap. He'll wake up some time later and block your punch or get out of the way. Throwing an overhead hammer fist while standing toe-to-toe with a guy is not only slower than Grandma going to town to get her Geritol, but he'll see it coming before you start. Now, if he's already messed up a bit and is a little out of it, then it can be used as a finishing blow. And it definitely will be a finishing blow if you come down with everything you have onto the bridge of his nose.

The place I liked to use this strike the most was on the ground. I liked to take a guy down and then start hammering away. I'd just work my arm like a piston that was out of control. That is where I found it to be the most effective.

It is also a very good blow if you have the guy doubled up in front of you, say from a kick or punch to the groin. A hammer fist driven down into the base of the skull or neck when someone is bent over is a very good way to put him face first into the dirt. And if he doesn't go down, you can easily keep pounding until he does. *A word of caution*: a blow with this power to the head or neck can cause very severe injuries!

I also like the hammer fist for spinning around and hitting a guy coming up behind you. Chuck Norris will use the spinning back knuckle often in his movies. This is just about the same, only I turn my fist so that the connecting part is the fleshy bottom part.

The only time I've ever knocked a woman to the floor was almost with this blow. I'll explain why I say almost. Things were flying every which way, and I was concerned with getting over to John and getting the two of us out of the area before the MPs showed up. I had just slammed a guy down onto the floor when someone grabbed my shoulder from behind. I turned and swung with everything I had, fully intending to knock whoever's head off with the hammer fist blow. As I was spinning, she came into view. Yes, it was a woman who had grabbed me. I don't know for sure, but I think she was trying to break things up and keep me from going back into the heat of things. It really wasn't her position to do this, but I can't hold that against her. When I realized I was about to clobber a woman, I opened my fist and lowered my arm so my open hand struck her in the shoulder rather than the side of the head. It still knocked her to the floor, but at least it didn't take her head off. Oops!

I have hit people in the head with that blow, and it does do some damage. If they are too close when you spin, you turn it into an elbow strike. If they back up and you miss, you'll be in a position to go from there. (Pay attention, defense tip here.) If they check you by jamming the shoulder and preventing you from spinning, pivot away from them to gain some distance between you and regroup. There is a lot of power out at the end of the arm after that big spin, but at the shoulder it can be stopped.

The Open Hand

Remember the old "Flintstones" episode where Fred and Barney went around doing the "Judo chop, chop!" Actually, the open-hand strike is a karate chop, but it was good for Fred and Barney. The real name is a shuto or knife hand. It is a useful strike in actual fights. I feel its best application is to the neck. The open hand can be delivered real quick, and you should wait to tighten your hand just before impact. Use the bottom or fleshy part of the knife hand as a striking surface. Some people like to hit elsewhere with it also, but I prefer it for the neck only.

The knife-hand strike to the back of the neck can be effective if you are behind him or he's bent over in front of you. More often, you will have an opening at the side of the neck. A knife hand to the side of the neck can momentarily knock a guy out. He won't be out for long, but long enough for you to have time for something else, like running.

The final target I would use a knife-hand strike to is the front of the neck. Right in the old Adam's apple. This is for serious situations only. You can easily crush someone's windpipe, and he'll die on you if he doesn't get a tracheotomy real quick. It doesn't take a very powerful blow to cause a lot of damage. So use this *only* in a life-or-death situation.

The other open-hand strike I like and will discuss a bit is the palm-heel strike. This is a very effective strike to use anywhere a punch would work, but there is less chance of hurting your hand with the palm heel. To deliver this blow, roll your hand back to expose the heel of the palm as the striking surface.

The nose and chin or jaw are good targets for a palm-heel strike. So is the solar plexus. A blow here will interrupt his breathing. Go over to the side a little and you can break the floating ribs. Right above the solar plexus is the sternum. (The bone in the middle of your chest.) This can be a useful target also. This same hand position can be modified just a little, and you have a claw to rake the eyes with.

There are a lot of things you can do with an open hand. Eye jabs are a very effective tool at times. You can flick the eyes with the fingertips, or you can drive your thumbs into the eye socket as far as they'll go. Just depends on the situation.

Another option you have is the slap. Everyone has heard of slapping or boxing the ears. This is a very good way to get someone to let go of you. Some teach to cup your hands and others teach you to keep your hands flat. Both ways will hurt and cause damage, possibly breaking the eardrum.

One time this navy puke ran into my truck (see Chapter 17, "Women,"), and I used an open-hand strike to floor the guy. (No offense to the navy. I have friends in all the services and respect them all. But I've also seen dirtbags in each of the services. This guy just happened to be a squid.) The first time I hit him was with my fist. And yes, it hurt a bit when I caught him in the mouth. So when he got up, I hit him a second time with an open hand. I struck him in the jaw with my palm. It knocked him back to the pavement of the parking lot, and it didn't hurt my hand at all. Later, my friend Matt said, "It looked like you only hit him with your open hand." I told him he was right and that if you do it correctly an open hand can do as much and more damage than a fist.

You can slap a guy with your open hand. This connects with the inside of your knuckles. It is more of an attention-getter. A palm strike uses the palm of the hand as a striking surface and delivers more power.

The hands are very versatile weapons in your arsenal. Besides the strikes, they can be used in grabbing, slamming, throwing, maiming, and all kinds of other stuff, some of which I talk about elsewhere. Learn how to strike with them from a variety of positions and situations.

One final word. You use your hands for many things every day, so take care of them. That's why I don't like punching so much. It hurts your hands at times. You break your hand and you can't work and you're out a paycheck. You can toughen your hands so they aren't as easy to break (by building massive amounts of calluses on them). But what girl wants to be caressed with hands like that? No, I'll keep my hands soft, thank you, and protect them while fighting. Then again, if you have a girl that wants to be caressed, what are you doing out there brawling?

KICKING

"Be it true or false, what is said about men often has as much influence upon their lives, and especially upon their destinies, as what they do."

—Victor Hugo

Les Miserables

At different times, I've spent time training in those fancy kicks you see in the movies. At one time I had a pretty decent jump spinning back kick. But I did this for fun! I've never even tried to use that fancy Kwai Chang Caine stuff in a real fight. Why? One, I like to be on the ground for balance. With one leg way up in the air, you are not as stable as when both feet are on the ground. Two, you shouldn't turn your back on an opponent unless there is no choice, like turning to get the hell out of Dodge. Three, I hope to have kids some day, and when one leg is up in the air your family jewels are pretty vulnerable. I'll talk a little about kicking in this chapter, but the most important thing you can remember is to never kick higher than your own waist. (I say your own waist because kicking a guy in the head is fine if he's on the ground.)[1]

After saying what I just did, I must add that high kicks are another thing you'll have to decide on for yourself. I don't recommend it, but I have seen people use them and come out on top.

My buddy John in Korea used to practice a lot of tae kwon do kicks, and he was pretty good at them. He stood six-foot-two and had a lean body. That's the right kind of build for kicking and tae kwon do. One night we were out prowling the streets of Tong Du Chong (sometimes Dong Du Chong), and we ran into a couple of people we knew. John and the one guy had had a disagreement about something earlier, and they started into it again. The guy squared off and made some comment about throwing down, referring to John as not having the balls to do it. John threw one of the nicest roundhouse kicks to the head I've ever seen. He snapped that kick out and struck the guy in the mouth. It didn't knock him down, but it sure staggered him. The guy's friends jumped in and held him up and pulled him away. I stepped over and kept John from throwing any more. They knew who we were, and the guy John had kicked out-ranked John. I didn't want him to get in trouble, and it was already decided who the victor was. And I'll be damned if John didn't kick him again as we were separating them.

So you can use those kinds of kicks in certain circumstances if you have trained and are proficient at them, and if you feel you can get away with it in the situation at hand. John was confident, and that night it worked for him. I've also seen John when his feet never left the floor. Most of the times he fought, he didn't use those fancy kicks. They are risky! Make your own choice on this one, but my advice is to stick with low kicks only.

There are a couple of kicks I believe to be the most effective on the street. These are the front snap kick, the front push kick, and the side kick. These aren't the only kicks you should learn, but these are the three I have used the most. The stomp is right up there also, so I'll discuss that one too.

The front snap kick is one of the basic kicks you will learn in a martial art school. It is delivered by cocking your leg by lifting up your knee and then snapping the foot out to the target. It is good for kicking the knees, the groin, and the solar plexus. I know the solar plexus is a little high, so it really depends on the height of the combatants. Dave, who trained in kenpo, showed the effectiveness of this kick one evening at a softball game.

The whole ordeal started over an insignificant event, like most fights do. After a couple of shoves, this guy charged Dave. He instinctively dropped into a ready stance and sent a front snap kick to the guy's solar plexus. It lifted the dude up and then down he went. Dave stayed in the ready and let the guy up. It was a softball game, and he didn't want to pound him. As it was, the guy charged again. Dave used the same kick to put him back on the ground. At this time, one of the guy's friends came up and tried to take Dave from behind. While Dave was concerning himself with the new opponent, others rushed over and broke everything up. Dave and the guy he dropped with the front snap kick were both ejected from the game, but it did show the effectiveness of the kick against a charge.

The front push kick is almost like the front snap kick, except that instead of snapping it out to the target and retracting it, you drive the cocked foot into the opponent's body and push him backwards. This is real good to get some distance between you. This kick is accompanied by a little hop with the foot that is on the ground. To see what this kick is like, get a heavy bag. Cock one leg up and put your foot on the bag, then hop forward with the other leg and push out with the one in the air. You should be able to play around with this and get to where you can do it to an opponent.

The side kick is just like it sounds. You cock your leg and drive it out to the side. You use the outer edge of your foot to strike with. The best target for this kick is the knee, if you want to do some serious damage to someone. It is also a natural if someone is beside you. I had a guy pinned against a wall one night when his buddy started to come up to help out. I snapped a side kick into his thigh and it bought me the time I needed to regroup and get my buddies into the ruckus. If I had placed the kick better it possibly would have stopped the guy for good, but I was off and only hit him in the thigh. This illustrates the importance of target selection. Often one well-placed blow will do much more than many misplaced shots.

The stomp is very effective if someone is down and you are still standing. It's just like it sounds; you stomp down on the guy. If you are wearing boots, this gets real ugly. I saw a guy on Hay Street in Fayetteville, North Carolina, get stomped and kicked one night by some biker wearing boots out in front of Rick's (a strip club well known to GIs at Ft. Bragg), and it was ugly. I only saw the very end of the ordeal, and I'm not sure what happened. But if the guy lived, I'd be surprised. Stomps like that to the head can be deadly. Stomping to any joints, including the hands, can put a guy out of the fight. So don't forget this sometimes neglected technique.

These are the kicks I recommend you become proficient at and practice. They are easy to learn and easy to execute in a real situation. Low round kicks like those the Thai fighters use can also be effective. In one of the Ultimate Fighting Championship matches I watched a guy wear down his opponent, who outweighed him by 90 pounds, with these kicks.

The only problem with this is that on the street you want to end it as quickly as possible, not just wear a guy down. But this kick can set your opponent up for a more devastating technique or blow.

In all actuality, the majority of the fights I have been in and have witnessed have had no kicking at all. Sometimes someone will throw something that remotely resembles some kick he saw in a movie sometime, and he will end up on the floor wondering what went wrong. It worked for the hero of the movie! Most of the time it is better to keep your feet on the ground. Balance is very important, and with one leg in the air it's harder to remain balanced. So usually I prefer to keep both feet on the ground, unless there is a real good opening that I know I can take advantage of—like the guy's on the ground and wanting to get back up and a boot to the head will keep him there. Animal shows a good example of this in the video *Barroom Brawling* with Peyton Quinn and Mike Haynack. When I watched that video I had to chuckle a bit and say, "Oh, I've done that." And if you find yourself on the receiving end of these kickball-type kicks while you're down, like I was the time my sweats tripped me up (see Chapter 18, "What You're Wearing"), roll and protect your head.

So there's my little spiel on kicking. I'm not much of a kicker, but you should train and use your legs to the best of your ability. As I've said, I'm an infighter and competed in judo. If you talk to a tae kwon do practitioner, he'll probably tell you a whole different story. He'll start by telling you how your legs are your most powerful tools and how you should base your training around these primary weapons. Who's right and who's wrong? Neither, it's just a different point of view. Check it out for yourself and come to a conclusion you feel comfortable with. I've given you my side, now make your own decisions.

NOTES

1. John actually had a guy tell him that it wasn't fair that he kicked a guy while he was down one night. When you're not in ring with a referee, anything goes.

INFIGHTING TOOLS

CHAPTER 9

Sergeant: "I'm a man of few words. If I

say come, you come."

Me: "I'm a man of few words, too. If I

shake my head, I ain't comin'."

Earlier, when I was discussing the ranges of fighting, I listed one range as infighting, or trapping range. Infighting is done from a very close range—that of a couple of inches to a foot or two. When you are this close, there are certain tools that are more effective and that you don't have available when you are farther away. I feel the best tools you have up close are your knees, elbows, forearms, and head. So I'll talk a little about each one, what they are good for, how to use them effectively, and how to protect them.

KNEES

Let's discuss the knees a little bit. One, the knees can be a devastating weapon in your arsenal. Two, they are a great target when you want to put your opponent down for the count. Three, because they are such a great target, you must protect your own.

Because I prefer to get in close, I like the knees as a weapon. They can do a lot of damage when you are up close to someone. The old knee to the groin works very well when you can get a shot in. The problem is that many guys automatically protect the groin first. It seems as though guys defend this area without thinking; you don't usually have to teach someone this. So kicks and knees to this area can be difficult to execute. Many times the best target to aim for is the one that is open and you can hit. Take what you can get, get it fast and hard, and then get out of there.

When the groin isn't available as a target, usually the thighs are. Down the middle of your thigh in the front is the femoral nerve, and a knee thrust into the thigh will result in a charley horse. This isn't a crippling blow, but it does hurt. Four or five thrown in succession will make it difficult for the guy to chase you, if nothing else. And it's a good way to set him up for an alternate and more devastating blow if needed. Remember, you will be doing other things to him as well. Don't expect a one-blow knockout; it's the combination of techniques that will do him in.

The outside and the inside of the thigh can also be good targets for knee strikes. Take what you can get. To hit the outside, if you are square with the opponent, hook your knee instead of going straight in with it. It's better to throw this after stepping off to the side. You don't really want to be squared up face-to-face if you can control the movement otherwise.

When you are using the knee as a weapon, you want to thrust your knee in, not up. Thrusting the knee in straight is stronger and not as easy to defend against. You need to lean your body back a bit as you thrust the knee in straight. You want to drive the point of the knee into the target. Use it like a Thai fighter does; they are exceptional at driving it in as well as hooking and driving it into the side.

If you are closing with the person, you can use the extra momentum to make the knee much more powerful. As you step forward with the opposite foot while closing, drive the knee deep into the solar plexus, ribs, groin, or thigh. Naturally, your height, his height, and what's open will determine which target is the best in each instance.

One circumstance where driving the knee up can be more effective than driving it in is when someone is bent over. A knee up into the face when a guy is doubled over is a good technique to send him to the floor. You can also drive your knee into his ribs while he's bent over. When you are real close to the opponent, driving the knee up into his groin is also effective, but still try to go forward too.

Some of these strikes are effective if you use the top of the thigh as well as the point of the knee as a striking surface. The most obvious example is the groin again. If you are real close and you drive your knee up between his legs, the top of the thigh might be the striking surface, but it will still do damage.

One other way to add a little to your knee strikes is to use your arms. The classic example is grabbing a guy behind the neck and smashing his face down into your knee as it rises. However, this is a finishing move or something you can do if you've just seriously sucker-punched the dude and he's still reeling.

Your knee and leg can also be used while controlling a person. When you have a guy pinned against a wall, use your knee and leg to keep his knees and legs pinned so he can't use them against you, like to knee you where you don't really want to be hit. A knee in the middle of a person's back or chest while he's on the ground is also useful at times.

The key to these, as well as everything in a fight, is the timing. You aren't going to just throw a knee into a guy's groin. If you try these moves too soon or at the wrong time they won't work. You need to look for the opening. When it's there, exploit it. When it's not, you need to do something to create the hole. Throw something up above, and when his defenses go up, hit him low.

Remember the movie *Roadhouse* with Patrick Swayze? One line I really liked was when, after kicking the guy in the knee, he told the other bouncers, "Give me the biggest guy in the world; you smash his knee and he'll drop like a stone." I was saying that way before I saw that movie (as were many other people). I used to always say that it doesn't matter how big a guy is or how strong a guy is, the knee is vulnerable. And no one with a messed up knee is going to catch you.[1]

Look at all the football players who have their careers ended by knee injuries. They are big, and they are strong, but the knee is a joint, and it doesn't matter how big your thighs and calves are—it is easily damaged, and when it goes it's all over. Most big guys don't guard their knees well enough. Remember this the next time you're facing a gorilla.

You don't need a lot of expertise in kicking to execute an effective kick to the knee. A stomping side kick or a front kick is all that is needed.

Since the knees are such a good target, you must take care and protect your own. You should learn to roll with a kick to your own knees. This is done by pivoting and turning your leg rather than keeping it straight so that it will snap.

You must also take care while training. I know this firsthand, so take note and learn from one of my mistakes. The worst thing about one of my knee injuries is that I did it to myself.

One evening at Ft. Bragg, Sam and I were throwing each other around the barracks. As I've said, I like to grab people and slam them against walls, and so on. Sam was bigger than I, so it wasn't real easy to throw him around, but that's what made it fun. As I grabbed the front of his uniform top, I was twisting to the left to slam him into a wall locker. One problem—I had brand new running shoes on and the floor we were on was clean and waxed. You know, the kind where your shoes will squeak. Well, instead of my foot pivoting as I was turning, the shoe stuck and my knee gave out. I didn't do any major damage; I just twisted it and did some minor tearing inside.

That "minor" tearing had me on the floor thinking that someone had ripped my leg clean off. It felt as if my knee had exploded. I spent a month on crutches, had surgery, and it was another five months before I could max the PT (physical training) runs again. So, watch your knees!

ELBOWS AND FOREARMS

A couple of favorites of mine are the forearm across the front of the neck and the elbow to the jaw. These are both tools that you need to be up close to a person to execute, but when you are, they work wonders.

The forearm has been called your own piece of pipe or iron bar. Although it's not quite that strong, you might think so if you were on the receiving end of one of those clothesline moves Steven Seagal uses in many of his movies. Properly done, these can be real effective. The forearm is also a great defensive tool. You can use the entire arm from the hand to the elbow as the striking surface when throwing a variety of circular blocks.

The last thing I like the forearm for is to press against someone's throat while he's pinned up against the wall. From this position you can easily drive your forearm up under his chin to snap his head back, or the more serious blow to the Adam's apple. The latter is only for very serious situations, and anytime you do anything to the neck and throat area you must use caution. A little will get the guy's attention; too much can seriously hurt or kill him. Usually, I've used this when I've needed people to see things my way. I wouldn't be out to hurt them at this point, just to make them understand my reasoning. When they became reasonable, I'd let them breathe again.

There was a time in high school when a friend of mine owed me some money, and he assured me he would pay me back as soon as this other guy paid him. No problem; I trusted the guy. A bit later, he came up to me and said he was real sorry. He wanted to pay me back, but since the guy who owed him money decided he didn't have to pay up, my friend didn't know when he was going to get back to me (he wasn't working at the time).

I said not to worry and that I'd go have a talk with the guy. One of the reasons he wasn't paying the money back was that he was a lot bigger than my buddy. He was a lot bigger than I was, as a matter of fact. I think that's why he ignored my first request to pay the money he owed. I asked my friend a couple days later if he had his money, thinking that my talking would have had an effect. "No," my buddy replied, "he told me to kiss off."

"OK, don't worry about it," I said. "I'll go have another talk with him." So later that day I caught the guy outside of school. "Hey, when you going to pay the money you owe?"

"Screw you!" he answered. Obviously, when I was younger I wasn't as well trained in negotiation tactics. So I reacted the way I usually did back then. I leaped at him before he knew what was happening, and I drove him back into a brick wall with a few good pushes. As his back hit the wall, I hit his front, slamming my body into his and driving my forearm into his throat. His eyes became very large as he listened to what I had to say. I let up just a little so he could answer "yes" to the question of whether he was going to bring the money the next day.

The key to this exchange wasn't so much the forearm to the throat as to my surprising him and acting so quickly. He wasn't expecting me to launch an attack since he was quite a bit bigger than I was. And once it happened, he was stunned, and with the lack of oxygen from my arm being across his windpipe, it didn't take much else for him to see things my way. My buddy, and then I, received our money the next day.

Up close, elbows can do tremendous amounts of damage to your opponent. They can be driven up under a dude's chin, or they can come straight across horizontally into the jaw, face, or neck. You can drive them down into the back of someone's neck when he is bent over, once you get him into that position. Yes, elbows can do a lot of damage.

I was watching some Thai kickboxers (muay-thai) in Bangkok one night, and in a flurry of elbows and inside blows, one fighter went down. I mean he went down asleep before he hit the mat. They came in with an old hand-carried stretcher, loaded him up, and carried him off so they could get underway with the next match. Those guys may be small, but they're as tough as nails, yet he'd been taken out by an elbow.

Anyway, the striking surface can be the back of the elbow near the triceps, or the front along the forearm. Even if the point you're utilizing is a damaging striking surface, you risk a greater chance of injuring yourself if you throw it against a hard part of the dude's body. What surface you will strike with really depends on what kind of strike you are throwing and what your target is. The best thing to do is some training on a heavy bag. Or better yet, wear some protective headgear and elbow pads and do some sparring and elbow work with your partner.

HEADBUTTS

The skull is the densest bone in your body. It has to be to keep your brain protected. But you can use this to your advantage when you are in close. Driving your head into the bridge of a guy's nose will definitely get his attention. You can also smash your head backward into the face of someone who is holding you. Sometimes this isn't easy to do, because experienced fighters look for this. But it is an option to look for if you are grabbed.

The key to headbutting someone is not to injure yourself. The actual connecting of your two noggins will do your opponent more damage than you, but what you have to look out for is injuring your neck. Don't just whip your head into his by using your neck. Drive your head into his face by putting your body behind it. Keep your neck immobile, and drive from your legs. I like to scrunch my neck down into my shoulders and drive with my torso. If you can grab a hold behind your opponent's neck and pull his face into the top of your head, you will increase the power of the blow. Remember, the skull is hard, so it's important to select the best target. Head-to-head hurts, but head-to-face is no problem. (As long as it's your head and his face!)

The headbutt can be a very good tool in your arsenal; just be careful when practicing and using it for real.

These are some of the best tools for fighting up close and inside. These, accompanied by eye gouges, finger pokes, ear slaps, and the like, will do a tremendous amount of damage while you're infighting. If you don't care for fighting in this range, use these so you can get back outside into the range you are comfortable with. But a couple of well-placed shots may just end it for you, so practice these and learn to defend against them so a well-trained infighter won't be able to do them to you.

NOTES

1. Marc says he always liked Sam Elliott's line from the same movie when Sam dropped the dude with a knee shot. He leaned over and smiled at the guy while saying, "God damn that hurts, doesn't it?"

TO THE GROUND

"What counts is not necessarily the size of the dog in the fight— it's the size of the fight in the dog."

—Dwight D. Eisenhower

Sooner or later, and more often sooner, you're going to hit the ground if you're fighting. More often than not, one or more of the combatants in a fight goes to the ground. The who, how, and when of getting there can make all the difference in the outcome of the fight.

All of the fancy kicks, punches, and other stuff taught in a lot of the martial art schools just don't work very well when you are on your back. They are especially useless if someone's on top of you. Try that spinning back kick when your face is smashed into the floor and your opponent's knee is in the middle of your back.

Oh yeah, I forgot to mention while he's pulling on your hair to put your head into a position so that his buddy can kick a field goal over the bar with it. Go ahead—use that well-practiced spinning back kick.

But when you're good at punching and kicking, you don't go to the floor. Yeah right, and the monkeys flying out of your butt will help you win the fight. I don't care who you are, if you fight, someone is probably going down. Not every fight, but quite often.

There are three possible scenarios: you are on the ground and your opponent is still standing; you are standing and he's on the ground; or you are both down. Of course, if you are fighting more than one person, it could be a little different, but that's another story. It's still going to be a variable of those three.

There are a number of ways to get to the ground. You might slip or trip like I did the time my sweats were wrapped around my ankles. This story is in Chapter 18, but for now just remember a time the phones caught you at the wrong time and you stumbled out of the bathroom to answer it with your pants still down. If you think it was hard to get to the phone, I'll tell you, it was a lot harder to get out of the way of a swinging metal bucket with my sweats around my ankles!

Let's get back to the ground. The next way to get to the ground is by being put there by your opponent. He can push, pull, trip, sweep, throw, or drag you down. This is probably the worst way to go down, because he is in control, not you. The next way is when you decide to go to the ground and you control it. The Gracies are excellent at this. They take people down for a reason, and they are in control while doing it. The last way to the ground is when it just happens. Neither of you planned to go to the ground, you just happened to end up there. This is real common in a lot of bar brawls. The fight just goes to the floor in a big pile of hitting, kicking, kneeing, elbowing, and anything else that the two of you may use to maim each other.

You can see there are a lot of possible ways for you or your opponent to end up on the floor and three different scenarios once one or both of you are there. It only makes sense that you need to include some ground training when you practice. This includes learning how to fall without getting hurt so that you can keep fighting or get back on your feet quickly as the situation demands. (The standard judo fall where you land and slap the mat isn't the best thing to do when your opponent is still wanting to stomp you.) You also need to know what to do in all three possible combinations. If you're up and he's down, you probably want to stay there. This is where you have the advantage. You can start playing soccer with the guy's head. (Some wrestlers and grapplers may go to the floor in this situation. But I think you'd be better off staying on your feet and practicing your field goals.) If you are down and he's up, you want to change the situation real fast or at least know how to defend yourself from this position. You definitely don't want your opponent playing soccer with you. If you are both down, the more you know about ground fighting and the more you've practiced, the better equipped you'll be to leave the victor.

FALLING

In the chapter "Walls, Stairs, and Such," I discuss how the floor or ground can be used real effectively to hurt your opponent. Why? Because it's very hard—much harder than your body. I can't recall ever seeing or hearing about someone's sidewalk being broken by someone's head. So, the most important thing to know about going to the ground is how to fall without getting hurt. People have fallen and smacked their heads on the concrete and died. It's that easy and that serious. If you've ever heard someone hit his head like this, you know it's a pretty sickening smack. I've seen people take blows that should have crushed their skulls and have nothing more than a headache, and I've seen other people die over a simple fall. Sometimes it's just a roll of the dice. Personally, I like to win, so I'll use loaded dice and protect myself when I go down. I advise you to do the same.

Learning how to hit the ground can help in situations other than fighting. I'm sure that my judo training aided me in jump school when I was learning PLFs (Parachute Landing Falls). In both, you learn to protect your head. It's also helped me in accidents. One morning I was running a little late, and I was trying to break speed records to make it to first formation in Korea. It was downhill, and I had my mountain bike going as fast as I could when a Korean man stepped out in front of me. (It was dark and I wasn't using my light, so it was sort of my fault.) Anyway, when I hit him I flew over the handlebars, him, and 15 feet of pavement before coming down on the blacktop. This was one of those times when you don't think, you just *do*. I landed by doing a forward roll and ended upon my feet. I was immediately at the Korean man's side to see if he was okay. He was, so I checked my bike and found only cosmetic damage. So less than 60 seconds from the time of my hitting him, I was on my way. Knowing how to fall kept me from getting hurt as well as keeping me from being late for first formation.

Notice how I said that the judo falls aided me—most importantly, in learning to tuck my head and prevent it from hitting the ground. If judo falls are all you know, you'll be better off than not knowing anything and landing on your head, but they aren't the best falls for a street fight. The roll I did after flying off my bike wasn't a judo fall. A correct judo fall would have had me roll and slap the pavement and stay down rather than rolling to my feet as I did. I didn't have time that morning to be lying in the middle of the street. In a fight, you definitely don't have time to lie around, unless you like getting your head kicked in.

It's important that you don't get hurt when you hit the ground—or that you at least minimize the damage to your body. (I'll talk about maximizing the damage to his body soon.) But you must also be able to get back up in a hurry. Remember the combination of you down and your opponent up? That's the biggie you don't want. You need to get back on your feet immediately. Rolling does this; slapping and stopping do not.

That brings us to the second part of falling. Take a brick and a ball and roll them both across the floor. What do you learn? Round things roll better, right? I know this sounds simple, and it is. But so many people ignore these simple things. If you roll that brick long and hard enough, the corners and edges are going to wear or chip off. The ball will roll a long time without showing any signs of wear. Your body is the same way. Your head, knees, elbows, and so on are the corners that are going to wear off, break, hurt like hell, etc. Keep them tucked and roll using the big parts of your body, and you'll minimize injury to yourself, which is what we're after.

The best way to learn how to roll is to get out and do it. It's just basic tumbling like kids do in gymnastics classes: the good old somersault, or forward and backward rolls. Practice forward and backward somersaults from the ground level first if they are new to you. Squat down, tuck your head, put your hands on the ground in front of you, and lean forward and roll over and come back to your feet. Then do the same with a backward somersault. Slowly get to where your starting position is higher. Soon you'll be able to dive over something and roll right up to a standing position again. This is what I did off the bicycle.

Backward is a little different from a standing position. It's real easy to do a backward somersault from the squatting position, but people forget that when they are standing. The most common reaction of people when they are falling backward is to stretch out their arms and land on both hands and their tailbone. This is a very good way to break a wrist. You can break bones with less than 10 pounds of pressure. Your body weight is enough to snap an arm easily. Even if nothing breaks, you're on your butt trying to get back up rather than already being there.

Before you practice backward rolls from the standing position, spend time doing the roll from squatting. When you are comfortable with this, then you can start to increase the height you start from. Once you get standing, practice it until it's a natural reaction. To practice, stand straight up. Cross one leg behind the other. I usually cross my right leg behind the left. Your weight should be on your front leg. Then just bend your front leg and sit down. Your back leg will act as a kind of shock absorber with the ground, and then you just roll backward. I usually go off to the side and roll over my right shoulder. Just go all the way over and back to your feet. *Important: Keep your head tucked!* You should keep your chin on your chest during the entire roll. Also important is to pull in your knees. Don't leave your legs straight. Remember to make yourself into that ball.

Another variation is to step back with one leg as you are going down and bend your knee. Doing this, you'll notice that it gets you close to the squatting position we started this with. Again, just tuck your head and your knees and roll. Practice going straight over and off to the sides. Practice somewhere soft at first, using mats or out in the grass. Once it becomes natural to you, you'll be able to roll on pavement without discomfort. (Too much discomfort, that is.)

Learning how to fall is extremely important. So get out there and practice a bit. It will save you more than once, I assure you.

BEING CONTROLLED (GRABBED)

At different times I've said I like getting close to a guy and slamming him down, and so on. The opposite of this is that I don't like anyone getting a hold of me. You shouldn't either. You want to be the one in control, not the one being controlled. And the most common way to control where a guy is going is by getting a hold of him. It's real common for a guy who starts to lose a fight to rush his opponent and grab. Watch for this and don't let him get away with it.

The best way to break someone's grip is to not give him anything to grab onto in the first place. That's one of the reasons it's so important to be aware and not let someone up on you. That's also why after the dance has begun we pull our limbs back as fast as we snake them out, and that's as fast as we possibly can. Don't leave something out there for him to get a hold of.

But because nothing ever works like it's supposed to, especially in a fight, you will find yourself at times being grabbed by your opponent. Remember all those ways a guy can put you on the ground? Many involve him first getting a hold of you so he can control where you're going. And the most common form of control used by the untrained fighter is grabbing you. If you are up against someone who is very experienced and has had a lot of training, he'll know a whole bunch of ways to control you, and you'll be in deep trouble if you don't know some counters yourself. (Remember, getting the hell out of there at warp speed is always a form of self-defense.)

For our purposes here, let's just look at the basic grabs and how to get out of them. The weakest point of someone's hand while gripping something is between the thumb and first finger. That is where you want to break loose from. When it's your wrist that is grabbed, you can use your arm as leverage and force your wrist out between the thumb and first finger.

87

Another common one is when someone grabs your upper arm and wants to force you in a particular direction that you may not want to go. Many people will start to pull away, and it ends up in a tug-of-war. Usually the aggressor wins these tug-of-wars because he's picked someone he can beat in the first place. This kind of grab is easy to get out of, but not by jerking away.

Have a friend grab you around the upper arm, and tell him to hold tight. Then take the arm that is being held and make a big circle with it, just like when you are loosening up your shoulders while warming up before some athletic activity. One big circle will usually break the hold, but if for some reason it doesn't, do another one. Once the hold is broken, you can determine what you want to do next—leave at warp speed or smash the guy. It's your choice once you're free.

Naturally, there are many other ways someone can grab hold of you. My best advice is to team up with a buddy and practice different grabs, holds, and escapes. Practice grabbing each other realistically, and practice ways to spoil the attacker's intentions. A lot of times we would go over a move until we had it down pretty good. Then we would speed things up a bit and see if we could get it to work. We knew the move that was going to be tried, so we worked on counters for just that move. We would see how we could mess each other up. This is very important for realistic training. Sure, you need to cooperate at times to learn the moves and techniques you're practicing. But in reality, your opponent on the street is going to be doing everything he can to ruin your well-laid plans. So, if you have encountered these possible counters, you'll know how they feel and be better equipped to handle them. I've seen guys lose it when a technique didn't work like it did in the dojo: "He wasn't supposed to do that!" Well, you'd better be able to regroup real quick, because more often than not, it isn't going to work perfectly.

Both partners get valuable training from this. The one who is doing his best to mess his partner's techniques up is learning what works and what doesn't for counters. And believe me, this is the place to find out! I've tried sneaky things in training that just didn't work. I'd find myself tied up in a knot or lying on the floor holding my balls. I remember one such time when the guy I was training with was flabbergasted: "You okay? I didn't know you were going to do that, and it was just a reflex to block. Your nuts were just there." Yeah, I guess that wasn't the way to counter that move, and I thought I was being sly.

TAKING A GUY DOWN

As I've mentioned, I like to close and I like to take people to the floor. There are many ways to get your opponent down, but nine out of ten times I would use the same method. It is sort of a variation of my favorite judo throw.

Back when I was competing in judo tournaments in Montana, I took a first place trophy home from a tourney in Missoula. That day, I executed a perfect throw in one of my five matches. In judo, a perfect throw is awarded an *ippon*, or one point. The match is over and the executioner of the ippon is awarded the victory. If that wasn't enough to get me to practice that throw even more, I was also finding that it worked to take friends down in our wrestling matches. So naturally, I resorted back to this familiar technique when things really counted.

I would take people down by shooting my right arm around their heads and putting them into a headlock. But I wouldn't stop there; I'd pivot into them and do something between a hip throw and just dragging them to the floor. I'd land on top of them with my arm still around their heads. They would be on their backs, and it was the perfect position to start pummeling them with hammer fists with my left hand. (After a couple blows, I could usually switch to my stronger right without worrying about losing my controlling hold.)

Besides this takedown, the next most likely for me to have used was the good old tackle. No finesse, no technique, just tackle the son of a bitch to the ground and make sure I landed on top. Neither of these methods would win points for looking pretty, but I really didn't care what it looked like. I just wanted to take the guy down and hurt him before he hurt me. Nothing else really matters when the dance has begun and bodies are flying.

There are a lot of good ways to take a person to the floor. You can put him there while you remain standing. Or you can take him down and go to the floor with him, but do it so that you end up in the controlling position once you're there. Learn and practice some of these. Get out there and toss each other around. I suggest you get real proficient at a couple of real basic takedowns. Practice doing them from different angles. What I mean is, can you come in from the side and still execute the takedown? From the rear? Starting from any position?

Along with these takedowns, you should learn some basic escapes and counters. Once you and your partner are proficient at both, you can really go to town on each other to see which ones you can actually apply. Just be careful with the real nasty ones. You want your partner training with you, not laid up with an injury.

BOTH DOWN

If you know how to fall properly and get back up quickly, you shouldn't have a problem with the you-down/him-up scenario. The key is not to let this happen. Remember, when you fall, get some distance between you and your opponent to give yourself time to get up. If by chance you are on the ground with him towering over you (not good, not good at all), you can roll away and get up (get that distance and time) or learn to kick from the ground. A well-placed kick to the knee of your attacker as he comes in on you will give you the time to get up and regroup.

If you put the guy down or he just ended up there, you have the advantage. A good boot or two to the head and then get out of there. No problem. Just watch out for him grabbing you to pull you down with him or kicking you in the knee.

So now we come to the scenario of both of you on the ground. This is very common, and the spoils of victory usually go to the one with the better ground fighting skills. There are a number of things you can do so that you fare better than your unlucky opponent.

The first is on the way down. If I'm going down, I like to take the guy with me. This makes sure that I don't end up in that me down-him up situation. The best way to do this is to grab the guy who's throwing you and hold on tight. Close with him and use your entire body weight to take him along for the ride. When you grab him, you want to try and control the outcome of the fall. I try to twist in the air so that I land on top. Of course this means that the other guy is on the bottom—the position that connects with that very hard ground we talked about. If it's his head or an elbow that hits first and breaks, the fight may be over right then. And you had his soft body to cushion your fall. Isn't that special!

I did just the opposite one time when I was messing around with some of my students in Japan. I was going down with one of them onto the wooden gym floor after he launched himself at me from the big climbing rope hanging from the ceiling. I didn't want to hurt him, so I twisted us in flight and took the fall on the large part of my back. This happened so fast I really didn't think about it (till I was lying there

going, "Oh, that hurt"). It reminded me why it was so important not to be the one on the bottom when you went down to
the ground with someone. We did this all the time when we
used to wrestle around. You didn't want to be on the bottom.
So it just becomes instinctive to try and twist and be the one
on top. Work at it and you'll see what I mean.

Now that you're both down there, you need to do one of
two things: do some damage to the guy so you can get up
before he does (and if you do enough damage, he won't be getting up) or put him in a restraining hold. In a street fight, I don't
recommend restraining holds. Just smash the dude and get out
of there (or at least get up to face his buddies). But in certain circumstances you aren't allowed to hurt people. The case where
my friend Dave, who was working night security at the dorm
where I was Resident Assistant, got in the middle of a campus
domestic quarrel is a great example (see Chapter 16 for the full,
unedited version of this war story). All Dave did was walk up
and ask if there was a problem, which was, of course, part of his
job, and the guy swung at him. If we had been downtown, I
would have slammed his head into the pavement a couple of
times and been on my way.[1] But because we were working, we
couldn't do that. So we controlled him until the cops arrived.
It's up to you to decide if you want to control or maim.

My favorite controlling hold is one where I get the person on
his back and I have an arm around his head. I'm sitting with my
back up against his chest and my arm wrapped tightly around
his neck. This leaves my other hand free to protect myself or to
administer pain in a variety of ways. If I take a dude down right
with my favorite takedown, I end up in this position. What a
coincidence. I can control or hurt. How convenient!

Of course, there are a lot of different controlling holds, and
you should learn some of them. You'll learn a lot about controlling holds when you are wrestling around with your partner, since that is what you will be going after most of the time

when you are on the ground. (You won't be using the eye gouges and such in your wrestling around.)

In the bar you just want to get it over quickly and get back to your feet. Punching is usually rather useless when you are rolling around. The only punches I throw on the ground are hammer fists when I'm on top. This is the only punch you can get some power behind from the ground. And to do that you need to be in the upper position. So rather than waste time trying to hit someone, go for the dirty tricks a ground fighter will use—nasty things like gouging, biting, and maiming.

Eyes can be gouged out, ears can be ripped or bitten off, and testicles don't fare well with a vicelike grip locked on them. These are the kinds of things you can do on the ground to hurt your opponent fast. I remember a friend of my dad's once telling me about a time when he grabbed a guy's balls and squeezed until they were coming out between his fingers. It definitely got the guy's attention. My buddy Greg had his thumb shoved into a dude's eye socket as far as it would go one night. All he was thinking was that he was going to put his thumb clear through the son of a bitch's skull before he let up.

Sure, this stuff sounds gross. Well, it is! Fighting for real is not a pretty picture. These are the kinds of things you need to do to survive in certain places. If you can't stomach the thought of biting someone's nose off, or ripping someone's ear off, don't go out fighting. This is what happens, and this is what works.

Again, with all of this you need to assess your situation. If it's a simple fight, maybe you don't want to maim a guy bad. Like if you know the guy and all he needed was a little attitude adjustment. But if it's for real, you need to get nasty. Get it over quick.

One last thing about being on the ground. I said you want to get back on your feet as quickly as you can. That's true, and you want to make sure your opponent doesn't get back up. I know that in all the movies the hero lets the bad guy get back to his feet so they can resume their choreographed dance. That's movies again, folks. Don't let your opponent back up. If you have him down, keep him there. I've fought people who were too damn big and strong to give a second chance. Once I had them, I kept going till it was over. If you let a guy back into the fight, he may just turn it around on you.

MORE THAN ONE

I talk more about this in the chapter on fighting more than one person at a time, but I felt it was important to mention here. If you are fighting more than one person, *don't go to the floor!* I've made this mistake a few times. You're dealing with the guy on the ground and the others start kicking you and smashing things down on your head. If you don't have someone to keep them off you, you're going to be in a world of hurt. A bunch of boots stomping your body can really ruin a night, or week, or life.

So remember, if it's more than one, keep your feet under you and remain standing at all costs. If you do go down, get up any way you can. Crawl under a table or anything else around to get away. Just don't stay there.

Ground fighting and floor work are valuable tools in the reality of street fights. The sudden craze over jujutsu has brought grappling arts into the spotlight. It will aid any fighter to learn to handle himself on the ground.

NOTES

1. Slamming someone's head into the pavement can do serious damage, depending on how hard you smack it. This can get you into serious trouble, so caution should always be used, or a less serious method of ending the conflict. I worded it this way because that's what I told the guy I'd have done if we were downtown.

CHOKES AND SLEEPERS

CHAPTER 11

"Force without judgment

falls of its own weight."

—Horace

Odes

When I was competing in judo in high school, I was choked out during one of my competitions in Plains, Montana. In other words, the competitor I was grappling with put a choke hold on me—actually a sleeper—and everything became real fuzzy super quick. The sleeper he used involves using the gi or uniform to help apply pressure to the sides of the neck, cutting the blood supply to the brain, resulting in everything blurring out.

About the same time, I read a magazine article on choke and sleeper holds. I started thinking there wasn't a thing I could do once that hold was locked on. I lost my strength and everything started to blur and fuzz out. Hey, that works, I should get good at that!

So I started to practice getting people in the most common—and what I feel is the most effective—sleeper hold. (I'll explain how to do it shortly.) We were always wrestling around back then, so whenever we started, my sole objective was to get that hold on my opponent, and I began to get pretty good at it. One time in a motel room at Myrtle Beach, South Carolina, I was wrestling with two buddies who were down there with me. (We often headed to the beach from Ft. Bragg when we weren't on DRF 1 or 9. DRF, or Defense Readiness Factor, is the status of alert the 82nd Airborne is on. If you are on DRF 1, you are the first to go if the unit is called into action. The unit that is on DRF9 would be the last of the nine battalions to go, but they are on two-hour alert status because they have to help the DRF 1 battalion leave.) Anyway, my sole objective during this match was to try to get both of my opponents into a choke hold at the same time. I had the strength advantage and the experience on these two, so I was finally able to get them both. I had an arm around each of their necks, and I started to squeeze. They both tapped out. Cool, I thought.

Later, I had opportunities to use these kinds of holds in real situations, and I was glad for all of the practice I had during those high school and army matches. I'll get to when I used them and how, but first let's discuss what chokes and sleepers are in the first place.

When you cut off the brain's supply of oxygen, a person will lose consciousness. If the restriction of this oxygen supply continues, brain damage and death will follow. There are two ways to restrict the oxygen flow to the brain; these are most commonly called chokes and sleepers. A choke is when you apply pressure against the windpipe or larynx to choke off the air supply into the lungs. A sleeper is when you apply pressure to the carotid arteries, which are located on the sides of the neck, interrupting the flow of blood to the brain and resulting in unconsciousness.

I personally like both methods for different reasons. One, I can control a situation without having to hurt the other person. This keeps you out of trouble with the law, as well as not having to hurt people you don't want to (e.g., someone in your dorm or company that you have to see on a continuous basis, or an out-of-control friend). Another aspect of these holds that I like is that they can get a person to listen to you. I'll explain shortly.

Extreme care must be used when practicing these moves as well as when using them in an actual confrontation. Yes, care must also be exercised when using these holds for real. I stated that a benefit was that you could control a situation without seriously hurting your opponent. However, these same holds can also kill. You must be in control of your own actions and use caution. This cannot be overstressed.

In judo, most participants "tap out" when a competitor gets them in a choke or sleeper hold. This is done by tapping the mat or the opponent twice in succession. There is also a referee watching closely to stop the match immediately in case of injury or unconsciousness. In practicing these holds, you probably won't have a referee. So use the "tap out" method and refrain from rendering your training partners unconscious.

When your partner applies a sleeper successfully, you'll know it's over as things start to get fuzzy. (It only takes a few seconds.) Tap something twice and quit fighting; if your partner doesn't let up, tap again. When your partner taps, release the pressure immediately. A few more seconds just for laughs can be dangerous. Train seriously and safely. I have never rendered a friend or training partner unconscious; I just don't feel it is necessary during training. We are out to have fun and help each other, not hurt each other.

There are two groups of chokes and sleepers, ones using clothes and those called naked chokes because you do them without the aid of clothing. I know some of the clothing chokes, and when a guy is wearing a judo gi they work very well. The time I was choked out in competition was with one of these. I don't care for them on the street, though. You can never be sure of what your opponent will be wearing and that it won't rip. So I like the naked chokes and sleepers for actual confrontations.

CHOKES

Let's discuss the choke. The choke I like and have used on many occasions is the one-hand front choke. This is performed just like it sounds; you grab the guy around the front of the throat and squeeze. A variation I also like to use is done by placing the bone of the forearm across the front of the person's throat and pushing forward hard with the guy's back and head against an immovable object. Walls work best, but cars, telephone poles, and such work also.

Remember, this is my preferred style of fighting. I like grabbing and slamming. My father was also this kind of fighter, and it was from him that I learned some of these methods of negotiation. This is of course when all other forms have been exhausted. Getting physical is a last resort, but unfortunately, some people only listen after you get their attention in this manner.

When I was younger, I used to play "mercy" with my father and always lost. He would also bring out the bathroom scale and we would each squeeze it and see who could squeeze the hardest. He'd then send me off to practice so that maybe one day I'd be able to beat him. He told me that developing hand strength was important for many things, one of which was, "When you have powerful hands and you grab hold of a guy, he tends to start listening."

Oh, how true. But something about being choked scares people, and you have to be cautious. Many times the person will stop and listen, and at this time you need to give him a little air. Sometimes, however, they will freak out and go berserk on you. It's scary not being able to breathe, and people will panic. If you've been trained in water rescue, you know what I mean. People who are drowning often go crazy out of fear. People you are choking may do the same, so you need to be prepared for them to just blow up and go full-out blitzkrieg on you. Having the strength to handle this is a great asset. This is why if you're not particularly strong it's better to go for sleepers.

The other common way to choke someone is from behind. Wrap your arm around the person's neck and place the bone of your forearm across the front of the throat, applying pressure to the larynx or Adam's apple. This pressure will block off the trachea and prevent the inhalation of air into the lungs. Unconsciousness is caused by the lack of oxygen to the tissues of the brain.

Chokes are the slower method of rendering your opponent unconscious, and the most hazardous. Too much pressure or a blow to the larynx or trachea could produce swelling, which could lead to suffocation. Extreme care should be used whenever using a choke hold, which is why they are outlawed by certain police forces.

SLEEPERS

"Burrese, Banister is pounding on Loftus!" came the call from an excited buddy. Jeff and I were usually called to break things up when ruckuses started in the barracks. So down the hall I ran to Sam's room. I found Russ knocking Sam around in the corner, while Sam tried to cover up.

I knew Russ had been upset and drinking, because he had been starting trouble earlier and I had talked him down. Well, this time there was no talking. I pulled him off of Sam and told him to settle down. He responded with an overhead cross toward my face. The alcohol had slowed him down a bit, and I easily avoided the punch and moved behind him, circling my arm around his neck to apply the sleeper hold I had practiced. I threw us both backward onto the bed in the room and locked it on tight. My buddy started saying, "He's turning colors, Alain." He relaxed some, and I released some of the pressure. I asked him if he was calmed down, and he replied that he was, so I let him up. He threatened me some by telling me I'd better watch my back, then went off toward his room to sleep off the alcohol. The next day he apologized, and everything was cool. Hey, Russ was a friend. We were usually on the same side, and we got all the Harlem Globetrotters autographs and pictures together. I was glad I could end the situation that night without anyone getting hurt.

Sleeper holds like the one I put on Russ work by applying pressure to the carotid artery. The carotid arteries run along the sides of the neck and are located straight down from the ear and at about the level of the Adam's apple. Applying pressure to these arteries is a faster and safer method of rendering a person unconscious than is a choke, but it too can seriously injure a person, so care should always be taken.

The way I like to apply this hold is to circle behind my opponent. There are many ways to do this, but I like to go to my left so that my right arm is the one used during the hold. If the person has just thrown a right, like Russ did above, you can spin him a little as you sidestep, block, and circle. Wrap your arm around your opponent's throat with your biceps on one side of the neck and the bone of your forearm applying pressure to the other. Use your other arm—in this case the left—to add to the pressure by pulling up and backward. I do this by grabbing my left biceps and, with my hand locked in the crook of my left arm, pulling up and back. Within a few seconds your opponent should start to lose consciousness. Apply the pressure until you feel your attacker's body go limp. Keep your arm in position after releasing pressure just in case he starts to fight again. You will be ready to reapply the hold immediately.

THINGS TO CONSIDER

When you put these holds on someone, he is going to be resisting. He will resist more from a choke than a sleeper, as I mentioned before, partially due to the length of time it takes for each of the two different methods to render unconsciousness. Be ready for this, and be ready to protect certain body parts.

Kicking back into the feet, shins, and knees is a common defense, as is striking to the groin. You can prevent these by taking your opponent down to the ground. Again, be careful while doing this with your arm around his neck.

The other targets someone will go for are the eyes and the hair. You can tuck your face down into the back of his head and withstand the pulling of your hair for a few seconds. So whenever putting this hold on someone, take him to the ground and tuck your face down.

This brings us to what you should do if someone tries to put one of these holds on you. The first thing is that you don't want an opponent behind you, but it will happen sometimes, even to the best of us. So if someone tries to get a choke or sleeper on you, get your hand in there. If you get your hand inserted between his arm and your neck before the hold has been applied, the target area (the front of the throat or the carotid artery) cannot be fully constricted. This will give you time to struggle and escape from your attacker. You must beat it before it is locked on; after that it is too late if the person does it right.

I put a sleeper hold on a training partner at Wolf's Karate Studio one night, and he called Mr. Wolf over and asked him what to do in a situation when someone had you in this hold. Mr. Wolf let me put the hold on him and then we started. He went for my legs and I took him down, he went for my eyes and I tucked my head. He ended up tapping out. "You're good at that," he said. Then he looked at my partner. "The best thing you can do is not let someone get it on you. If they do, you're in trouble."

It is a very good idea to learn resuscitation techniques. In most cases a person will regain consciousness in a few seconds to up to a few minutes. It depends on many factors specific to each individual. It is just a good idea to know how to resuscitate someone who has been put out. This is one reason I never put out a partner or friend while training. Why take the chance of something going wrong? I wanted to practice fighting, not first aid. (Here is an interesting note: many of the greatest warriors also studied the healing arts along with anatomy.)

One time in Korea, I used a sleeper against a loud-mouth. My squad leader witnessed the ordeal and yelled to me not to kill the guy. (Yes, he was concerned that I might.) When it was over, we had a little talk. He told me he liked what I had done. I showed the guy who was boss and shut his mouth without seriously hurting him. The guy knew I could have done all types of damage to him when I had him at my mercy. But all I did was show him who was who. No one was hurt and no one got into trouble. My squad leader said as far as he was concerned it was over if I said it was over. I said it was and nothing more was said. (Except for all the stories of Burrese "putting out" Cervi that circulated for a bit.)

Chokes and sleepers are just a couple more tools in your repertoire of techniques. Learn them and they may be of some use someday when you need them. They are effective, but they must be used responsibly. Be careful, practice safety, and hopefully you'll never have to use one.

TRAINING

CHAPTER 12

"Train more than you sleep."

—Masutatsu Oyama

The Kyokushin Way

There are a number of skills involved in fighting, including punching, kicking, throwing, and all of the other things you can do to hurt your opponent and keep him from hurting you. As with any skill, improvement only comes through practice and training.

There are numerous martial arts that teach skills for sport and combat. There are also many things you can do that wouldn't be considered art, but they get the job done when your life's on the line. I'll talk a little about martial arts. Then I'll discuss how you train and things I think you should incorporate into any martial type training, whether in a classical martial art, or if you and your buddies just get together to beat on each other for your training. I personally like this last form of training. Nothing like having a friend smash your head into a brick wall to teach you that you don't want this to happen when it really counts. More on this later.

First, I want to emphasize that I respect all of the different forms of martial arts and those who train in them. However, just getting a black belt from a certain school does not guarantee that you will be a competent street fighter. There are many black belts who would get stomped by people who have never been in a traditional dojo and have never had any so-called training. They learned it all the hard way, by stomping and getting stomped.

I have personally studied judo, kempo karate, tae kwon do, toshikan karate, and hapkido. My problem was that I was always moving around, so I could never stay with one school long enough to earn the high-ranking belts. I think all of this training helped in different ways when I was fighting in the bars and on the street. Because of my build and personal preference of style, I think the judo training helped me the most. As I've said, I like to close and slam people into walls or to the ground. Judo training fits right in with this type of fighting.

So, if you are interested in getting some formal training in one of the many martial arts, go for it. But if you want to be able to handle yourself on the street, be sure that your training incorporates the principles I talk about in this chapter. If it doesn't, your black belt may only be good for holding up your pants.

When selecting a martial art to train in, there are three important terms to be familiar with. Doctrine, strategy, and tactics are important related components of each martial style.

The martial doctrine of a style is the set of broad beliefs that the style is based on. The strategy of the style is the plans for fighting based on the doctrine. Finally, you have the tactics, which are the specific techniques used to carry out the strategic plans.

I'll use tae kwon do as an example. The doctrine or beliefs that this system is based on is one of the legs and feet being your best weapon. So the strategy is to fight in a kicking range, with a stance that you can easily launch a kick from. The tactics are the numerous kicks that are taught to the tae kwon do student.

Before you select an art to train in, you should evaluate your strengths and weaknesses and choose an art that fits with your body type and is appropriate for the kinds of threats you may face.

Remember to not get locked into one doctrine or style. Sure, the tae kwon do guy does great in a big open area when he can keep his opponents away from him. But if a jujutsu man takes him to the ground, all his kicks are useless. If the art you study doesn't include training for all ranges of fighting, supplement your training. Be prepared to fight in any range. A skilled fighter controls the range of the fight; however, at times you can't, and you need to be ready for those surprises.

There are a lot of books and magazines that tell about the different arts. Peyton Quinn does a good job of describing the different martial arts and their application and self-defense value in his book *A Bouncer's Guide to Barroom Brawling* (published by Paladin Press). This book has a lot of other good information and advice from a guy who's been there. It's well worth reading, and I recommend you check it out. Study a variety of martial arts publications and check out a few schools. After you decide what you are going to study, the important thing is how you train.

The old saying "the more you sweat, the less you'll bleed" is true. You need to train hard with actual physical contact to become effective on the street. It's a sad fact that many schools

that say they are teaching self-defense and fighting skills pro-
mote students to high levels when they have never actually hit
one another. Hitting a person is a lot different from throwing
a punch in the air or stopping it short of contact in sparring. It
is different from hitting a heavy bag, too.

You also need to encounter getting hit. People react differently when struck. Knowing what it's like to take a punch
reduces the fear and shock that may arise during an encounter
on the street. Of course you must exercise caution when training. If you send each other to the hospital you'll be without a
training partner. But you do need to incorporate some full-
contact training, with precautions and safety measures, into
your program. So let's discuss the important ingredients for
any training.

TRAIN HARD

I'll say it again: the more you sweat, the less you'll bleed.
You need to train hard and for real. I remember a time in
Korea when Ike and I were knocking each other around. We
were going at it pretty good when this lieutenant came running over, yelling at us to break it up. He thought an actual
fight was going down. We stopped, and Ike, who was about
six feet and 210 pounds, looked at him with this sheepish grin
and said, "We were only playing, Sir."

Now, of course you can't train like this every day. Well,
maybe you can. It seems like these matches broke out whenever we didn't have anything to do. But when you are practicing techniques, you need to go slower at a controlled pace
to learn them properly and to avoid injuring each other.
Then you should work to where you practice these at the
highest level without injury. I'm saying injury, not pain.
There's a big difference. Certain pain in training is good, if
not absolutely necessary. Pain, like many other things, is

something you can get better at dealing with. But you need to experience it first. If you don't want to deal with any pain, I suggest you forget all about this fighting bit. It hurts when it's for real, and to be prepared you are going to hurt in practice.

A Little More about Pain

An important thing to do while training is to train through certain pain. When your buddy hits you good in the family jewels and you're doubled over on the floor, it's always nice when he stops for a moment and checks to see if you're okay. This won't happen in the street. Your opponent will be all over you when you're at your weakest. So when these things happen while you're practicing or messing around, keep going. Don't stop till later.

Ike and I were going at it one day when he slammed my head into a brick wall, hard. He stopped, and even though I was seeing stars I managed to say, "Keep going." So he did. I knew it was a good training opportunity to practice with my head spinning, and boy was it. I ended up having a knot on my head the size of a golf ball and a headache for quite some time. Ike was definitely the winner of our match that day. Learn to push on through nonserious pain.

When it comes down to serious injuries, which happen even though you try to avoid them, you need to stop immediately and administer first aid and get the proper medical attention. Sam and I were bouncing each other off of walls and wall lockers one day at Bragg when I twisted my knee. I had on brand new running shoes, and the floor was freshly waxed. So instead of my foot pivoting, it stuck and my knee gave out. The guys in the barracks got me to the hospital quickly, and I ended up having to have surgery and all that fun stuff. I guess I don't have to say much more about new shoes and waxed floors.

Just as in weight training, there is pain you train through and there is pain you need to listen to and stop and possibly get medical attention for. Learn the difference and train accordingly.

THINK WHILE TRAINING

Always be thinking while you are training. Think of how things would apply on the street. Notice what works and what doesn't. There have been many times while training or messing around that I've zigged when I should have zagged. This is how I know that it's nice when your buddy stops when you're on the floor holding your groin. Learn from these mistakes.

Animal and I were doing some knife work one morning when he stopped the basics and said, "Now what are you going to do?" He had this gleam in his eye and was coming at me with the training knife. It looked real ugly. I was wishing I had a sniper rifle and 500 meters or more between us. But since I don't carry a sniper rifle around with me much any more, I answered, "Grab a chair." That's what I'd do in a bar.

"Well, there's one sitting over there. Why aren't you grabbing it," he snarled. I moved toward the chair and he cut me off. So I jumped behind the heavy bag that was hanging there, and when he came for me I swung the thing up into his face. An 80-pound bag to his face gave me the few seconds I needed to get to the chair. His reply, "Good, you were thinking!"

For a while, one of my roommates at Bragg was a wrestler, and he was good. He would tie me in knots at times. I always tried to make sure he couldn't get the same hold on me twice. Unfortunately, he always came up with different ones. Pay attention to what works and what doesn't. Learn your own weaknesses and work to improve them. Help each other correct mistakes and point out the weaknesses of your partner.

The more of this kind of training and thinking you do in practice, the better you'll be when it's for real. With the proper training, you don't even think about what you have to do when you get into a real situation. It becomes automatic, and often it's hard to remember just what or why you did something; you just did it.

LEARN A VARIETY OF SKILLS

Eric had a saying at sniper school—"You can teach any piece of shit to shoot, but you need it all to be a sniper." This is so true. Shooting, or marksmanship skills, is only one element of the training of an effective sniper. What good is a guy who can hit a target from 1,000 meters if he can't find the target in the first place?

Fighting is the same way. You need to know how to handle the situation in a variety of ways. You have to be able to fight in the different ranges. You need to know how to use all the tools you have available and which ones to choose in each particular situation. That's why I said it is good to supplement martial art training with different styles. Someone who practices judo should also learn how to punch, kick, and use the other options available besides the trips, throws, and grappling moves that judo is based on.

The last important skill I'll recommend you practice is that of escaping. Practice running down alleys, jumping fences, going around cars, and so on, before you have to do it for real. I was lucky that in the army we had obstacle courses and such to practice these skills. We would also run through the woods for some of our morning PT sessions. Dodging trees and limbs, jumping fallen logs, and avoiding all the other pitfalls of the woods is good training for when you need to exit a place in a hurry. I used to run through the forest all the time when I was a kid in Montana, so I had a leg up on a lot of guys when we did these runs in the army. I still remember the words of one of my drill sergeants, DI Hernandez, and you should, too. "I can roll left, and I can roll right. If need be, I can low-crawl up the middle."

PUT SHUGYO INTO YOUR TRAINING

The samurai had a very rigorous and severe training regimen called *shugyo*. It is the act of driving yourself past the levels of endurance you previously thought possible. It can be done in many different ways. Anything that takes you to the limits of your physical and emotional capabilities can be used as shugyo training.

We used to do this long before I learned the Japanese word for it. Warriors of all types throughout the ages have engaged in tests to find their limits. Do you know yours? You never will until you test yourself. And you'll find that with determination and guts, you can go longer and farther than you ever imagined. We used to call it a ",gut" check. We'd say, "It's mind over matter: you don't mind, it don't matter." The army gave us chances to do this with the extended road marches, competitions, and other training missions. If you told many people to go hike 30 miles over a steep mountain, they would say, "I could never do that." Well, I've done it and I know I could do it again if necessary.

I remember Greg entering a marathon one time: "It's a mind thing, just to do it." It was the same reason I stayed up for 73 straight hours without any stimulants besides some coffee (and not very much of that). I did it just to do it and see what it was like and how far I could go. Those are the things you need to do once in a while to see where your limits are. Only by finding these limits will you be able to train so that you can surpass them.

Don't go out and injure yourself. Greg was in shape when he entered the marathon. If you're in bad shape, you could go out and put yourself in the hospital with a heart attack. Push yourself to your limits and beyond, but do it intelligently. Only you can determine where these limits are and how far past them you want to go.

This kind of training thrown in every once in a while will build your confidence and increase your determination. That willingness to keep going. The ability to get back on your feet when your body is yelling, "Stay down, stay down!" is critical for surviving when things get serious. Sheer guts and determination have saved many a person in life-and-death situations.

* * * *

These are just a few suggestions to incorporate into any training regimen. Train hard and for real, think, train for variety, and test yourself every so often. Remember the maxim "Tomorrow's battle is won during today's practice."

FITNESS

"The word 'aerobics' comes from two Greek words: aero, meaning 'ability to,' and bics, meaning 'withstand tremendous boredom.'"

—Dave Barry

Stay Fit and Healthy until You're Dead

Everything I've talked about in Part Two concerning "getting physical" is based on being fit. Yes, it's true that smaller men and women can defend themselves against dangerous assailants with proper training and technique. But don't believe the claims that size and strength don't matter. Strength and aerobic conditioning are vital to helping you come out of a dangerous situation the victor.

Dispel any illusions you have about technique making up for fitness. The simple truth is that the stronger, faster, more agile, and more durable you are, the better your odds of surviving in combat. Many times I've come out on top simply because I was in better shape. I outlasted my opponents.

In actuality, it has been my level of conditioning that has saved me in tight situations more than technique. Grabbing a guy and slamming him against a wall isn't a common technique taught in martial arts classes, but if you have the strength to do it, it sure is effective at times.

It just makes sense that the better conditioned you are, the better your odds of surviving a hostile threat. I once read an article by Mark Londsdale saying that the best thing you could do for self-defense training is to get started on a running program. You can increase your running ability a lot faster than your fighting prowess.

I used to always max the PT tests in the army, and I'd always tell people that it wasn't just to get a good score that I stayed in shape. Slamming, jamming, and escaping require you to be in top form. The weights I threw around in the gym helped me throw people around when necessary. Lots of pull-ups helped when I needed to climb a fence or pull myself up onto a roof. Tons of push-ups enabled me to throw tons of punches before my arms started to fatigue. And maxing the two-mile run came in real handy when most of the MPs couldn't. (I'm sure a lot of MPs were in decent condition, but my conditioning and knowledge of the area always ensured an escape.) Being able to run was also very useful when you woke up downrange (off post in Korea) and were late for formation.

Now that I've bragged a bit and illustrated the importance of being in shape, let's look at what you can do to increase your level of fitness. Now that I'm certified by the International Sports Sciences Association (ISSA) as a Fitness Trainer, I train and speak to people on many areas of fitness and training. There are many variables involved as to what kind of program is best for each individual. This chapter is only a very basic primer on health and exercise. There are many good sources of knowledge on training and fitness, and I encourage everyone to learn more about this subject and incorporate a fitness program into their lives. Not only will it increase your odds of surviving a physical encounter, but it will reward you in many other ways too.

If your occupation requires you to become physical, or you just seem to get into jams a lot, it is all the more reason to be in top physical condition. So let's get started.

COMPONENTS OF FITNESS
AND THE PHYSICAL ATTRIBUTES NEEDED FOR FIGHTING

What is fitness, anyway? Fitness actually incorporates a variety of factors and is not the same for everyone. Different occupations, life-styles, genders, and ages create different sets of standards for fitness.

A lot has been written on fitness and wellness, and at times the two have been interchanged. I personally believe that for people to live in optimum health they should incorporate a wellness program in their lives. Wellness includes physical, emotional, spiritual, intellectual, vocational, and social dimensions. For the purposes of this book, I am only going to discuss one dimension, physical fitness.

Physical fitness deals with all things concerning your physical body. This includes exercise, diet, and medical care. Again, there is a lot of information out there on this subject. I'm just going to give you the basics on exercise and nutrition that will help you in the "combat zone."

First, let's look at some of the key physical attributes that need to be developed to make you a more competent fighter.

The first is power. Power is an essential ingredient in the fight game, especially if you rely on forceful movements such as punches, kicks, or judo-type throws. (Yes, I know that technique is better than just powering a guy over. But on the street, it's nice to have some power also.) Power is different from strength, because strength is only one component of power. Power equals mass times speed. Mass is determined by your size and your ability to lever between the ground or some other solid object and your target. Speed is how quickly you can deliver that mass to your target, which is determined by your strength and flexibility.

What this means is that to increase the power of your techniques, whether they are punches or whatever, you must increase your size, strength, and speed. Increases in size are rather difficult. You don't want to become larger by gaining fat, and muscle-building is a long and slow process after you acquire the quick gains of a beginning weight lifter. So training for strength and speed are the key ingredients to increasing your power.

Since I already mentioned speed, let's look at it as the second important attribute of a fighter. In this sense, I'm talking about how fast you can physically move rather than your reaction time. As I mentioned, speed is one of the components of power. The faster a punch, the more powerful it will be. But remember you need the mass also. That's why a lightning-fast jab with just your arm won't knock a guy down. But a super-quick punch with your weight behind it or moving with it (mass) can floor a guy.

Learning proper technique with tons of practice will increase your speed. You learn to contract the muscles needed to perform the technique and to relax the antagonistic muscles, or those that are counterproductive to the desired motion. An example is relaxing your biceps and letting the triceps do its work throwing a punch. But you can also condition for speed by building strength and flexibility.

The next attribute you need to be an effective fighter is endurance. It's true that most real fights only last a few seconds, and the stamina of the combatants doesn't come into play. However, facing multiple attackers, escaping and evading, or any other unforeseen mishaps may call on your endurance reserves. The greater these are, the better you will fare in the situation. Especially when it goes to the ground and you don't really want to maim the person.[1]

You will also need a fair level of stamina to undergo any form of rigorous martial training. If you are training like I suggested in the previous chapter, you'll need endurance. Actually, those hard training workouts will help increase your stamina and endurance levels to a degree, but I also recommend some form of alternate cardiovascular workout.

Your stamina depends on two factors—your muscular endurance and your aerobic condition. Muscular endurance can be broken down into strength endurance, local muscular endurance, and speed endurance. Your aerobic condition is determined by your cardiovascular and cardiorespiratory endurance.

Strength endurance is not as critical to fighting. It is your ability to generate a single all-out effort (known as "limit strength") over and over. An example would be a power lifter. He needs strength endurance to perform single repetitions lifting maximum poundage several times throughout the day of competition.

Local muscular endurance is the kind of endurance most needed when fighting. This is being able to perform sustained, submaximum muscular contractions over an extended period of time. Earlier, when I mentioned doing many push-ups in order to throw many punches, I was referring to building local muscular endurance.

Sprinting is the most common example of speed endurance. It's the ability to continue contracting your muscles at maximum intensity. This can be extremely important in the E and E (escape and evasion) phase of your encounter.

117

Cardiovascular endurance refers to the efficiency with which you get oxygen to your working muscles while, at the same time, removing metabolic wastes. In short, this is conditioning of your heart, lungs, and circulatory systems. Besides keeping you going during a physical encounter or enabling you to run like hell to get out of the area, cardiovascular fitness is a key ingredient to health and the prevention of heart disease.

The fourth attribute I'll discuss is agility. Agility is the ability to combine strength and dynamic balance in performing a series of directional changes in rapid succession, where dynamic balance is the ability to maintain control of your body's center of gravity while moving. In other words, it's your ability to move quickly and easily.

With agility comes the attribute of coordination. If you develop all of the components of physical fitness and practice the skills you wish to perform, you will develop your coordination, or fluidity of movement. Grace and power combined result in coordination.

While discussing these attributes needed for fighting, we touched on the different components of physical fitness and exercise we need to engage in to become proficient at handling physical encounters. We need to train for cardiovascular fitness, muscular strength, muscular endurance, and flexibility.

Yes, the number-one way to improve your fighting is to fight, by engaging in training like I discussed in the previous chapter. But that's not enough! You should participate in a thought-out fitness program that includes all of the components of fitness. Only in this way will you reach your full potential and be as prepared as you possibly can for any encounter.

I also believe that you should embark on a program that emphasizes balance. This has been something I have stressed throughout the years I have been training, and it is due to this training philosophy that I was able to come through many encounters successfully.

I used to max the two-mile run on the PT tests, but I didn't always come in first. There were quite a few guys that could outrun me. But those guys couldn't bench press 300-plus pounds like I could. And yes, there were some big mammoths who could outlift me in the gym, but none of those guys could keep up with me on the obstacle course. And when it came to pull-ups and push-ups, there were few who could match me. A balanced and well-rounded approach to training was and still is very important to my training, and it should be for yours too unless you are training specifically for a certain sport or event where you have to emphasize one aspect of fitness over the others. Some athletes are actually not "fit" in some of the components of fitness. If you want to win marathons, you won't be building your muscle mass with weights. And if you want to lift maximum poundage in a weight lifting competition, running will hamper your training for this sport. If you engage in a specific sport, you should rely on your coach's competency to guide you toward the best training to ensure maximum performance during competition. However, for general fitness, and to be ready for any encounter you may face on the street, I advise a well-rounded, balanced program of exercise.

THE OVERLOAD PRINCIPLE

Before we talk about training the areas we have determined to be important to our level of fitness, we need to understand a basic principle of training.

The most basic and important principle to advancement in physical fitness is the overload principle. Simply put, you must continue to subject your muscles to more stress than they are used to in order to make gains in strength and endurance. This increase in the amount of stress can be done in two ways: you can add volume or you can add intensity.

Adding volume can be done in a number of ways. If you are weight training, you can increase the number of repetitions, the number of sets, or the number of exercises for the muscle group being trained. You can increase the volume of your aerobic training by running, swimming, biking, or hiking longer distances.

Adding intensity can be achieved by lifting heavier weights or performing more difficult exercises. Decreasing the rest time between sets or exercises also adds to the intensity. The intensity can be increased in your aerobic training by going at a faster pace or by engaging in interval training.

Remember, this is only a primer, and I'm only giving you the basics here. If you are unfamiliar with any of the exercises I mention, it is important that you are trained properly. Do not begin any exercise program without proper instruction from someone educated in the field. These basic guidelines should be adapted to your own level of fitness and education. Some of you will be reading this and saying to yourself, "Duh, who doesn't know that." Others don't have any prior exercise knowledge, and this will be new to them. It is also important that you know your physical condition before beginning any rigorous exercise program. If you're in doubt about your condition because of years of inactivity, play it safe and see your doctor before beginning.

TRAINING FOR MUSCULAR STRENGTH AND ENDURANCE

The most effective method of building strength is through progressive resistance training. This can be done through lifting free weights or training on any of the numerous machines designed to create resistance for specific muscle groups.

Just as strength training is one component of a balanced

fitness program, you must have balance within your resistance training. Your strength training program needs to include exercises for all parts of your body. Don't imitate those who only train their biceps to impress people by showing off their flexed arm. You need to train everything! The bonus is that those impressive arms will come with everything else.

Here is a list of the body parts you should include in your program and some common exercises that work each muscle. There are many other exercises to choose from, and I recommend that you do some further reading to expand your knowledge in this area.

Upper arms: Everyone likes training the upper arms. These are the muscles that look good in a T-shirt. The upper arms have two main muscle groups: the biceps, which bend your arm, and the triceps, which straighten your arm. Even though it's the biceps that we flex when we want to show off our arms, it's the triceps that make up the biggest muscle mass in your arm. If you want big arms, you need to train them both. Remember, punching power comes from the triceps and shoulders. Work everything!

Biceps:
> All forms of curls—
>> Barbell curls
>> Preacher or Scott curls
>> Dumbbell curls
>> Concentration curls
>> Hammer curls

Triceps:
> All forms of extensions—

Triceps extensions
Overhead extensions
Triceps press-down
Dips
Close-grip bench press or push-ups

Forearms: I mentioned the importance of strong forearms before. They are used for grabbing, pulling, pushing, and gripping.

Reverse curls
Regular wrist curls
Reverse wrist curls
Gripping exerciser

Shoulders or deltoids: Your shoulders are used to raise your arms as well as lift things overhead. I've put shrugs here also. Actually, shrugs work the trapezius muscles or "traps." Those are the muscles in the middle that pull your shoulders toward your ears.

Overhead press or military press
Lateral raises
Front raises
Shrugs
Upright row

Chest: The chest is another popular muscle because of the ever-popular bench press. Any pushing movement requires a strong chest, and if you are on the bottom of a pile when things go to the floor, a strong chest will aid you in pushing your opponent off.

    Bench press
    Incline bench press
    Fly (all types)
    Push-ups
    Pullovers
    Pec-deck fly

Back: The back is a large area and is responsible for a lot of the power exerted in certain movements. A strong back is crucial to prevent injury in the pulling, pushing, twisting contortions you put your body through during a physical encounter. In addition, the strength needed to throw someone around often comes from a strong back.

Upper back—latissimus dorsi:
    Pull-ups
    Lat pull-downs
    T-bar rows
    Bent over rows
    Single-arm rows

Lower back:
    Low-back extensions
    Seated cable row

Abdominals and obliques: The abs and obliques make up your stomach and sides. They are important stabilizing muscles for most movements.

Abdominals:
    Seated knee raises
    Leg raises
    Hanging knee raises

Crunches—knees bent
Crunches— knees up
Reverse crunches

Obliques:
Side leg raises
Side jackknife
Side crunches
Side bends
Seated or standing twists
Leg-overs

There are also a number of machines that require you to do crunch-like movements for the abdominals and twisting movements for the obliques. Some people prefer these machines and others do not. Try them out and see for yourself.

Legs: Strong, powerful, explosive leg strength underlies excellence in many athletic endeavors. Fighting is no exception. Strong legs provide stability in your stance, they enable you to run or jump, and they provide power for kicks and stomps. The legs are most easily divided into three groups to be trained: the quadriceps or quads, which are the upper front of your leg or thigh; the hamstrings, which are the upper back portion of your leg; and the calves, or the back portion of your lower leg.

Quadriceps:
Squats
Front squats
Leg extensions
Leg press
Lunges

Hamstrings:
> Leg curls
> Standing leg curls
> Stiff-leg dead lift
> Good mornings

Calves:
> Standing calf raises
> Donkey calf raises
> Seated calf raises

Neck: The neck muscles are often neglected when doing strengthening exercises. Because they hold your head in position, you will prevent many unnecessary injuries from happening by ensuring that the muscles of your neck are strong. You can use head straps with weight as well as just using a towel. A training partner can hold your head while you push to both sides and forward and backward. Be careful when training the neck. Don't "force" any head or neck movements; you want to strengthen your neck to prevent injury, not cause one yourself.

Now that we know all the body parts to be trained, we need to put together a program that will ensure that each body part is brought up to its potential. Remember, this needs to incorporate the overload principle I mentioned earlier.

Much of your training will depend on your personal goals and objectives. Naturally, the more you train and the better physical condition you are in, the better you will perform in all physical endeavors. This includes fighting or running for your life, whichever the situation calls for.

The minimum I recommend for weight training is to work out the entire body three times a week. You should have at least one day of rest between each training day. Typically, a Monday-Wednesday-Friday training schedule is used.

You should pick one or two exercises for each body part and do from 5 to 10 total sets for each specific muscle. Work the larger muscles such as the back and chest first, and then move on to the smaller muscle groups. If you exhaust your biceps and triceps first, you won't be able to handle the weight needed to build your chest and back.

To build muscular strength you should use a weight at which you can perform 6 to 10 repetitions each set. To build muscular endurance you should use a weight that you can perform 10 to 20 repetitions each set. Since both are important, I recommend that you mix up your training on different days. On Monday and Friday of one week you may want to lift weights in the 6 to 10 rep range, and on Wednesday of that week use lighter weights for high reps. Then on alternate weeks you can do a couple of days of high rep work and one day of 6 to 10 rep training. Again, it will depend on your level of fitness and your desired goals.

I also like to include some "heavy" days in my training. On these days I lift weights that I can only do 1 to 4 reps with. I, like many others, like to know what my max on the bench press is. When you are performing these heavy lifts, it is important to keep good form, and you must be extra careful not to injure yourself. You should also never perform heavy lifting without a spotter. I recommend only doing these heavy days once every two weeks or so—once a week at the most. Too much extremely heavy lifting can be taxing on the joints.

Remember balance; vary your exercises and the poundage. This variety will keep your routine interesting and help prevent burnout and overtraining.

Of course, there is much more to be learned about weight training than I have put here. You may want to gradually advance to more complex routines and techniques to shock or stimulate your muscles to adapt and grow stronger. There are many ways to do this, and all of them are built around the overload principle—that you must continue to apply more stress to the muscle being trained by increasing the volume or the intensity.

Each person needs to determine his or her own fitness goals and strength-training requirements. Then you can tailor a progressive resistance routine into your overall fitness program that meets your personal needs and objectives and coincides with your life-style.

Proper training will ensure that you have the muscular strength and endurance to carry you through your training as well as seeing you through an actual physical confrontation.

MORE ANAEROBIC TRAINING

Weight training is the most common form of anaerobic training, but I think it is good to include other forms also. (Anaerobic means "without oxygen," remember?) We know that most fights are very quick. You must be able to engage in maximum energy output for a short burst of time (or multiple short bursts as the situation demands).

One of the most famous and common forms of this type of training is Fartlecs, named after the coach who introduced the training technique to world-class runners. It is also called interval training. You simply alternate jogging and sprinting. So you jog a little distance—300 to 400 meters or so, and then pour it on for a hundred-meter sprint. Make sure you give it your all. Then you jog a little more. You keep this alternating up for a desired time or distance. Our track coach would make us run Fartlecs for 40 to 50 minutes a session.

You can use this same principle in any of your other training activities. It doesn't have to be running exclusively. Just add short bursts of maximum intensity into your other activities.

AEROBIC CONDITIONING

Everyone has heard about aerobics. What this term means is simply "with oxygen." So an aerobic exercise demands large quantities of oxygen for prolonged periods of time. Aerobic exercises such as running, biking, swimming, walking, skating, and such have been shown to provide significant health benefits. My grandfather just turned 86, and he walks two miles a day. He cites this walking as the reason he's still running around the country enjoying life.

There are many sources of information out there on aerobic conditioning. Kenneth Cooper is probably the most recognized author and authority on aerobic conditioning, and I recommend you do some further reading in this area also. It is beyond the scope of this book to include complete conditioning programs, so as with the weight training, I'll just give you a couple of bare-bones guidelines.

Before you start an aerobic conditioning program—or any type of exercise program—make sure your body is up to it. As I said earlier, it's a good idea to get a thorough medical examination before embarking on any exercise program. Only you know your current physical condition and what you have been doing to keep in shape.

The key to improving your aerobic condition is to perform an aerobic activity that will maintain your heart rate at a level to achieve a training effect. To do this you need to reach your target heart rate and keep it there for a desired length of time (at least 20 to 30 minutes).

Your target heart rate is determined by taking a percentage of your maximum heart rate (MHR). The most common formula for determining your MHR is by subtracting your age from 220. While training, you should have a heart rate of between 60 and 80 percent of your MHR.

Next, choose a basic aerobic exercise like the ones I mentioned above and go to it. You should train for at least 20 to 30 minutes a session three to four times a week to gain significant results. Get your heart pounding in the desired range, and keep it there for the required time.

Aerobic conditioning is important for general health and fitness, and it is crucial if you are going to live a life-style that involves getting physical.

WARM UP AND COOL DOWN

It's not a good idea to jump into strenuous exercise without warming up a bit beforehand. Cold muscles do not perform as well, and there is a greater chance of tearing a muscle while the muscles are cold. Of course, in an actual confrontation this is exactly what you are going to do (jump right in without a warmup—not tear a muscle). But when you have a choice, you should warm up for 5 to 10 minutes before going on to more strenuous work. The simplest and probably the best way to warm up for workouts that involve continuous movement, such as running, swimming, cycling, and such, is to just begin your workout slowly. With these aerobic sessions, you shouldn't get your heart rate up past 50 percent of your MHR for those first 5 to 10 minutes. Then you can increase your workload until you are in the desired training effect range (60 to 80 percent of your MHR).

You should also warm up before beginning a start/stop exercise session such as lifting weights. Riding a stationary bike for 5 to 10 minutes will do the trick. Then you can perform a light first set of each exercise to further warm up the specific muscles you're about to use. This will reduce your risk of injuring yourself. Many people used to think that doing some stretches was an adequate warmup. It's not. It is actually not good to stretch your muscles while they're cold. Do that

129

5 to 10 minutes of light activity before you do your stretches if you want to stretch some beforehand.

At the end of your exercise session, you don't want to just stop cold. Collapsing on the ground after a strenuous high-intensity exercise session is one of the poorest ways to recover. You need to spend another 5 to 10 minutes doing a light aerobic cool-down activity. Let your heart rate return to normal gradually. This is the time to do some stretching. Ideally, you should do 5 to 10 minutes of cool-down activity followed by 10 or more minutes of stretching.

STRETCHING

All individuals need a certain level of flexibility. How much flexibility one needs is determined by the person's activities. Many traditional martial artists are very flexible. They can do the splits, and they can do all those fancy high kicks. We discussed that you shouldn't really be kicking above the waist, so you don't really need to be that flexible.

So how flexible should one be? That depends on you. I have never been real flexible, even though I worked at it when I was participating in formal martial arts classes. That doesn't mean you shouldn't stretch, it just means that you don't have to have the flexibility of a world-class gymnast or martial artist. I do believe that the more flexible you are, the less chance you have in sustaining certain injuries. This is especially true when you have to leap into action without a warm-up, as is the case in street fights.

I do recommend that you include some stretching in your fitness routine. The best time is right after you have completed your workout and cooled down. This way your muscles are warmed up already. You don't want to stretch your muscles while cold. This stretching after your workout will also aid in recovery and will lessen the post-exercise soreness. I also like to do some stretching while watching TV at times. Just jog in place for 5 or 10 minutes to warm up (shadow boxing and the like work also). Then do some stretching while watching your favorite program or movie.

Remember not to bounce when stretching. Make your movements slow and easy. It shouldn't hurt or be too uncomfortable. Go easy and gradually. The most common method of stretching is "passive stretching." This is the simplest and safest form of stretching. It's the basic stretch to the desired position and hold for 10 to 60 seconds. There are many books and articles out there that describe the different positions, so I'm not going to list them here. Just remember to stretch all parts of your body.

There is a new method of stretching that I've been looking into called Active Isolated (AI) stretching. Robert Arnot, M.D., talks about this form of stretching in his book, *Dr. Bob Arnot's Guide to Turning Back the Clock.* AI stretching is being used more and more by Olympic athletes and deserves some further study. I recommend that you check into this if you are serious about becoming more flexible.

NUTRITION

I have done a lot of studying in this field and believe it to be very important to one's level of health and fitness.

It only makes sense that the better the fuel that you put into your body, the better it will run. You need the food to get you through your grueling workouts and to give you energy for all of your other activities. It is a combination of sound nutritional habits and exercise that will keep the fat off the middle of your gut. Having low body fat levels not only makes you look more attractive, it allows you to move better also. It also makes it easier for the planned withdrawal, or E and E stage, if it comes to that.

There are many books and magazine articles out there on nutrition, and there are opposing views by equally qualified experts. Since each of us is different, with a variety of activity levels and fitness goals, there isn't one specific diet to meet everyone's needs. What I'll do here is give you a few basic guidelines.

The FDA recommends that you try to limit your total fat intake to about 20 to 30 percent of your calories consumed. It suggests that your carbohydrate consumption should make up 50 to 60 percent of your daily calories, and protein should make up the remaining 20 to 30 percent.

An example would be the following:

Daily calorie consumption = 2,000 calories

400 calories from fat (20%)
1,000 calories from carbs (50%)
600 calories from protein (30%)

Go easy on the real fatty stuff. Fats are important, but most Americans eat far too many. Even if you try to limit your fat intake, you will probably be getting more than you think. That's why I take more of a bodybuilding approach and shoot for a lower percentage than the FDA recommends. Try to choose "good" fats like those from olives and nuts, rather than saturated fats like those from animal sources and palm or coconut oils.

There is some controversy about a high carbohydrate diet, and whether, like a diet high in fat, it will also lead to obesity. With carbohydrates, again, the kind you eat is a key factor. The type of carbohydrates you consume affects your blood sugar levels, and that in turn affects the fat that accumulates around your waist and other parts of your body. The ones to avoid are the fast-burning sugar carbohydrates that include products made of white flower like white bread, pancakes, bagels, and cereals; soft drinks; desserts; muffins; and donuts—and obviously, all of those candy bars that line the counter by every cash register. (Many of these are also high in fat.) The slow-burning carbohydrates are the ones that should comprise the largest part of what you eat. These include cereals such as dried grits, oatmeal, and other whole-grain cooked cereals; legumes, such as beans, lentils, and split peas; whole grains, such as barley and wheat bulgur; and vegetables, such as peas, asparagus, and broccoli.

The last of the three is protein. How much do you need? This topic too is surrounded with controversy. I tend to agree with those who claim that athletes or those with more active life-styles need more protein than your average person. The amounts recommended vary from source to source, but one guideline from *Fitness: The Complete Guide*, edited by Frederick C. Hatfield, Ph.d., states that "athletes require anywhere from .925 grams to 2.0 grams of protein per kilogram of body weight per day."

Foods that are high in protein are eggs, milk, meat, and fish. You must be careful, though, because many of these foods are also high in fat. Some of the lower-fat sources include skim milk, egg whites, chicken and turkey breast without the skin, and tuna packed in water. When buying red meats, look for the extra-lean types and remember to trim the visible fat off before cooking. The variety of protein powders you can find at most health food stores offer another readily available source without the high levels of fat. (I frequently use these in my diet for their convenience, and I will mention them more in my discussion of supplements.)

It is recommended that you divide your food consumption into five or six smaller meals a day, rather than the old standard of two or three large ones. Even though this is a healthier way to eat, I find it hard to do sometimes. So a couple of my

133

smaller meals are comprised of supplement bars or drinks. I find this much quicker and easier to fit into my busy life-style. Each of your meals should be well balanced and include a variety of fruits and vegetables to ensure that you get the required amounts of the essential vitamins and minerals. A good rule of thumb is to ask yourself what you're going to be doing physically until the next meal and eat accordingly. If you'll be sitting in the office without much activity, you'll want to eat less. If you'll be engaging in a high level of physical exercise before your next eating session, you should eat more.

Another very important but often neglected aspect of healthy nutrition is the consumption of water. You should drink 8 to 10 glasses of water each day. These should be spaced throughout the day, not downed all at once. Don't wait till you are thirsty, just get into the habit of drinking water throughout the day, and especially before, during, and after a strenuous exercise session. You can substitute fluid replacement drinks for some of these 8 to 10 glasses, but nothing beats good old water. Coffee, tea, and soft drinks should not be substituted, as caffeine and sodium negate the positive hydrating effects of water.

It's important to remember that these are just guidelines (and basic ones, at that). It is what you eat over a period of time that is important. If you pig out at the local buffet with your friends once in a while, it's not going to kill you, or, for that matter, make that big of a difference in your health or weight. (Although this is not the healthiest way to eat, I, too, enjoy a good buffet.) However, if you do this five times a week for several years, the cumulative effect will become visible around your midsection. So try to eat sensibly and follow sound nutritional practices, but don't be afraid to indulge yourself once in a while.

When it comes to food supplements or sports foods, there are two opposing views. Some believe that supplementation will aid performance, enhance recovery, and provide necessary nutrients lacking in the diet. The critics believe that the only thing these products enhance is the manufacturers' profit. They claim that a person can get all of the nutrients needed for optimal health by eating well-balanced meals throughout the day. This may be true in theory, but how many of us eat the proper number of well-balanced meals? That's why I believe in using supplements. Many times I'm busy and on the go, so I don't have time to eat what I'd like. I find it very convenient to drink a protein shake or eat a sports nutrition bar to get some added nutrition without added fat. These products aren't meant to be meal replacements, but they are good to tide you over until you can get the next meal. Many days, I just don't have the time to stop and eat five or six meals. So three good meals and two or three protein drinks or sports bars spaced throughout the day ensure that I'm getting everything my body needs.

There is enough research out there supporting the belief that the active, athletic person needs increased amounts of some nutrients, and that some sports foods aid in sports performance. I also side with those who claim that a person building muscle through weight training has increased protein requirements. I use supplements often with my training programs and have found them to be beneficial. The times I have pushed my bench press poundage up over 315 pounds have also been the times I have consumed the most supplements. Whether it was physical, psychological, or both, I feel the carbohydrate drinks I was consuming before and during the workouts and the protein drinks I was drinking after the intense training aided in maximizing my lifts.

You will have to decide which, if any, supplements to use with your training program. The ones I have found useful are the following: 1) protein powders after workouts and sometimes at other times of the day; 2) carbohydrate and sport drinks when I'm thirsty and want something other than water; 3) the various energy or sports nutrition bars on the market, such as MET-Rx bars, when I don't have time to eat a meal (they are handy and easy to take with you, even if you don't care for the taste); and 4) a multivitamin and mineral supplement. I don't use any of the herbs and related supplements that you see lining the shelves of health food stores. I stick with the four basic kinds of products I've listed.

Since I don't have the space to go into great detail about the different supplements, their uses, and their benefits here, I recommend that you do some further research on this topic if you are serious about maximizing your physical potential. *Dr. Bob Arnot's Guide to Turning Back the Clock,* by Robert Arnot, M.D., has a good section on sports foods. He describes the different types of products out there, explains what they are for, and lists a number of specific products with their pros and cons. I also agree with his approach to nutrition and exercise, and I highly recommend this book.

Your body is a high-performance machine, and the fuel you put into it will affect its performance, just as the type of gasoline affects a high-performance engine. Proper nutrition will not only make you feel and look better, but it will provide you with that extra energy when you need it, and that's what really counts. Fighting requires the use of your body to its fullest. Only by taking care of it with proper exercise and nutrition will you reach your peak levels of performance. I don't know about you, but if something gets serious, and I'm in the middle of it, I want my body to perform to its maximum capacity to get me out alive. So take care of yourself and stay in shape. Even if you never fight again (wouldn't that be ideal), you will be better equipped to handle any other situation that arises as well as just being able to have more fun and live a longer and healthier life.

NOTES

1.   If you want a good workout, try one of C.J. Caracci's fitness tapes. If you can hang with him, you're in good shape. *The Navy SEAL Workout Challenge* is his first tape, and *Burnout PT Challenge* is his second and more advanced tape. I recommend both.

OTHER IMPORTANT INGREDIENTS

"Pay attention to detail."

—Gy. Sgt. Carlos Hathcock

There are many things to consider beyond just the physical aspects of combat and fighting. A number of contributing factors determine who the victor will be in any given encounter. In this part of the book, I want to look at some of these considerations—things like the friends or women you're with or what you're wearing. We'll look at fighting drunks or more than one opponent at a time. I'll also discuss different weapons and using environmental aides such as the floor or walls. But first I'll talk a little about the most important variables there are in determining who the victor will be—

specifically, the mind of the combatant and the speed and ferocity he utilizes during the encounter.

THE MOST IMPORTANT INGREDIENTS

CHAPTER 14

"The ablest man I ever met is the man

you think you are."

—Franklin D. Roosevelt

Are there any Rambo fans out there? I have to admit, I like Sylvester Stallone, and I liked the *Rambo* movies. Granted, they weren't realistic, but they were fun. One line that I really liked and believe to be true was in the second movie, *Rambo: First Blood 2.* It's where he states that the mind is the most important weapon. Nothing could be more true! You can even order a poster from the Delta Press, Ltd., catalog with the saying, "Your Mind Is . . . Your Primary Weapon." This saying surrounds the heroic figure of a Special Forces soldier.

Your mind is the most important ingredient in how you will come out of any violent encounter. Your mind controls everything else you do. Naturally, it's your mind that enables you to learn the different techniques and strategies to employ during a confrontation. And it's your mind and thinking that enable you to be aware of your surroundings—and how you are affecting your surroundings—in order to avoid trouble in the first place. But I'm going to talk a little about your actual mind-set and attitude during the encounter, as well as some other mental considerations. This will be a key to your survival. It has been shown that we only use less than 10 percent of our brain's power, and if we could learn to use more, the limits of our abilities would be unimaginable. Our minds are undoubtedly our greatest tool or resource when it comes to anything. Protecting yourself when engaging in physical confrontations is no exception.

BELIEF

A person's beliefs have the power to create and the power to destroy. Why does one woman fight off several attackers and another quietly succumb to their aggression? Much of this has to do with the person's belief system.

If you don't think a person's belief system is important, you need only look at some of the cultures that believe in voodoo and witchcraft. People actually die from their beliefs in these black arts. Look at all of the monumental events in history that have been accomplished by peoples' belief in religion. A person's beliefs are powerful.

Basically, a belief is just a feeling of certainty about something. So here's what I want you to be certain about: NO ONE HAS THE RIGHT TO DO YOU BODILY HARM! As crazy as this seems, some people don't share this belief. There are certain individuals who believe that they deserve to be hurt or that others have the right to do them bodily harm, and they allow themselves to be victims. Some battered women fall into this category, believing that they deserve the beatings from their spouses, or that their husbands have the right to do what they are doing. These women may also find it more difficult to fight back against a stranger, for they have been conditioned to accept violent acts against them. This kind of thinking is sick, and it disturbs me greatly. This is not the belief system we should be following. You must have the belief that no one has the right to do you harm, and this is true for men, women, and children. (It goes without saying that you shouldn't harm anyone else unless you are absolutely forced into it. And then you must go all out to the degree that's warranted.)

When my father was a boy, he came home after being beat in a schoolyard fight. When his father asked him if he had won, he replied, "No." My grandfather then proceeded to give my dad a lickin'. Dad figured he got whipped because he had lost. So the next time he got into a schoolyard tussle, he made damn sure he won. He didn't want to get licked twice in the same day again.

When his father asked him if he had been in a fight, Dad answered, "Yes."

"Did you win?"

"Sure did," my dad replied. Grandpa Ben then proceeded to give my dad another lickin'. Dad said he really wasn't sure why, and it bothered him. So a little later he went back and asked Grandpa Ben to talk.

"Sure, what's on your mind?"

"Well, I don't understand it. When I lost, I got a lickin'. And when I won, I still got a lickin'."

Grandpa Ben smiled a little and said, "You can't figure this out? The point is you're not suppose to fight. That's what the lickin's are about."

"When is it okay to fight?" my dad asked his father, knowing that he had also been in fights before.

"No one has the right to put their hands on you. If they do, you have the go ahead to mop the floor with them."

My father followed this standard throughout his life. Even though he engaged in quite a number of battles, the other guy always started it. (There are times, though, when you can say the right thing to get the other guy to swing first. Then it's open season on the unlucky one that got stupid with you.) My grandfather instilled this belief into my dad, and Dad then gave it to me. I now want to give it to you. Make up your mind right now that no one has the right to do anything to you. You need this belief so that you can develop the next mental component, determination.

DETERMINATION

Friedrich Nietzsche wrote, "He who has a why to live for can bear almost any how." This brings us to the fact that determination to live and to win can overcome a lack of size, strength, and skill. The why to live should be obvious, and we have already instilled a belief that no one has the right to take that away from us.

On my "sniper" jacket that I had made up while I was in Korea, I have this saying: "It's not the skill to win, but the will to win." I believe this wholeheartedly. I have beat people based solely on my physical condition and my determination to win. When I asked my dad one time what the single most important thing that determined the outcome of his fights was, he replied, "I just set my mind to the fact that I would not lose. I didn't think of anything else, and I didn't feel anything. My sole purpose was to defeat anyone I was against." My father reads a lot more about European and American history and military leaders, while I look more toward the Asian doctrines. His words reminded me of Mataemon Iso, who said, "Approach the moment with the idea in mind that you're in the fight to the finish." Different backgrounds and teachings, but the common theme of determination.

The football coach Mike Ditka once said, "There's something that makes a great athlete great. And I'm not sure it's physical talent. I think it comes from within." I'll say it does, Mike. There are many who have the physical potential to become great in athletic events who fail due to the lack of will power or determination needed to achieve superior standing in their sport. Then there are abundant stories of those who overcame severe handicaps and difficulties to rise to the pinnacle of success. Sheer guts and determination got them there.

You must cultivate this determination within yourself. You must be totally committed to the accomplishment of your goal. If you cultivate this trait in all of your activities, it will carry over into the area of self-preservation. You must be determined to win if you are put into a situation that involves your becoming physically aggressive. In other words, when you realize and decide it's time to fight, you'd better be determined to give it your all, no matter what.

This determination comes from accomplishing goals and realizing that you can do anything you set your mind to. When I was in high school, my dad gave me a shovel and the keys to his pickup. My chore was to move dirt and gravel from a nearby gravel pit to fill in the driveway that we had encased in a wall of railroad ties (the collection of the ties is a whole different story). Anyway, I was working on this project during the summer and after school in the fall.

Finally, I had moved enough dirt and had completed the task. Dad took me to the gravel pit, which was part of a small mountain. "You see how big of a chunk of that hill you took out in the last month or so?" he asked. I nodded and he continued, "Now, you weren't working all that hard—some during the summer and a little after school—and you still moved a hell of a lot. You see, a man can move a mountain with a shovel if he puts his mind to it." And he was right. The hard part for most people is putting their minds to it.

These kinds of tasks will help you build determination. It also helps if you are very competitive, as I have been throughout my life. I hate to lose at anything, and a fight is no exception. When I was younger, this trait would often lead to overzealousness in friendly competitions or games. I've since learned to be more socially agreeable, but I still don't like to lose. And when something really counts, that fierce competitiveness is there waiting to serve me.

The last method that I found to be helpful in being committed and determined to win was thinking of heroes or role models. The two primary figures that filled this role for me while I was younger, and still today, are my father and the fictional character Tarzan. I read all of Edgar Rice Burrough's *Tarzan* novels when I was growing up; in fact, I read them over and over. Now, Tarzan was someone who didn't give up, no matter what odds he faced. So often, when I found myself in a difficult situation, I thought of how Tarzan would never quit, and how he went through much worse hardships than I was going through. I would think of my father the same way: "Dad wouldn't quit."

Yes, thoughts of Tarzan and my father helped me find the strength to keep going on many occasions, including physical confrontations. You need to find your own models to use, and this can be done in a number of ways. It may be by emulating a hero as I did with Tarzan and Dad. It may be the thoughts of loved ones that give you the drive to continue through a nightmare that you find yourself in. Determination is often intrinsic, but a stimulant of some sort to aid you in difficult situations can bring out the sheer will needed to make it through.

Some of you may find this is not entirely to your liking. Well, it works for me. There may be other things you can concentrate on to bring out the best in yourself; the object is to find something that works for you. It's not so much how many times you get knocked down, but how many times you get up.

The relentless determination to never fail or lose will bring you out of more confrontations than any of the physical skills you may learn. Mastery of the physical skills is definitely important, but it will be to no avail if you don't have the determination to back it up.

ATTITUDE

When you possess the belief that no one has the right to do you any harm and the determination to see through any task you set your mind to, it will be easier to adopt a survival attitude. This attitude or mind-set is of vital importance when you are engaged in a battle where the loser will be lucky to be breathing when it's over.

You have to accept the reality that you will have to hurt another human being. This is actually very difficult for some individuals. When you go into combat mode after you have tried all other alternatives to fighting, you must enter it with 110 percent of everything you have. You have to be ruthless and have the mental toughness to put every ounce of strength you have into neutralizing your opponent. You mustn't go into it half-heartedly. For whatever reason, you're in it now and you mustn't hesitate. Your attitude of ruthless aggressiveness, backed by the determination and commitment to not lose, will be a strong determining factor in who will be the victor of the confrontation.

Stay Cool

Often you'll hear people say that you need to get mad when you're in a confrontation. Or someone will say, "When I get mad, watch out!" We even saw this in *Rocky 3*, when Paulie said to Apollo, "He's not getting killed, he's getting mad." I'll agree with this train of thought to a certain degree. But, it has to be controlled anger.

I went down in a pile once outside of my barracks in Korea. I got into it with a few guys from a different platoon, and I was going to town. They had me outnumbered and were all over me, so I was hitting whoever I could. They were guys from my company, so this was a fight and not combat. I wasn't throwing throat shots or trying to maim people seriously, and they weren't out to kill me either. Naturally, it didn't take long for some guys from my platoon to join the ruckus and start pulling bodies off of me (see Chapter 20, "Fighting More than One," for more on this). The point I want to make is that I didn't hit any of my platoon members. I was angry, but I was in control. I knew what I was hitting and refrained from striking any of those who were trying to break it up, and I had the sense to not throw blows that would seriously hurt people. You always have to remember the difference between fights and combat.

The out-of-control fighter with head tucked down and arms a flailing is always easier to beat than the fighter who keeps his cool and uses controlled anger to his advantage. This self-control is not only used to control your anger but to control your fear also. Fighting is scary. When you're outnumbered or outgunned it can be damn scary. I know tougher men than I who admit they soiled their pants in certain circumstances. But you mustn't show it—or let it hamper you in any way. You must control this fear and do what has to be done.

Learning to remain cool comes easier to some than others. It seems that some individuals just naturally face emergencies and difficult situations with a level head, and others freak out at the stupidest things. Just going through emergencies will increase your ability to remain cool. The first-time intern may lose it when an emergency patient is wheeled into the ER, but the experienced doctor just goes to work and does what he needs to do to save a life.

Athletic competition will aid a person in gaining the ability to stay calm under pressure. Joe Montana was definitely smooth and level-headed when he was out on the playing field. If he hadn't had the ability to remain calm under the immense pressure he faced, he never would have led his teams to so many victories, ensuring himself a place in the Hall of Fame as one of the all-time great quarterbacks in the NFL.

Behavioral scientists have discovered that the mind cannot tell the difference between events vividly imagined and those actually happening. This discovery led to a lot of work in visualization to increase athletic performance. If you vividly imagine stressful situations and confrontations where you remain cool and level-headed, you will increase your ability to do the same when it's for real. The key is to actively play out the entire scenario in your mind. Vividly see all of the happenings in your imagined situation. Visualize it realistically and work with possible solutions to things that may go wrong. Think of things your opponent may do to mess you up and what the realistic options in that case are. Don't just visualize yourself Bruce Leeing a whole herd of attackers without a scratch to yourself. That's not realistic visualization. For this drill to be useful, you need to do it like all other training. Train for realism and train for the Murphy factor—things will go wrong. This prior thought will better prepare you for an actual emergency.

Staying cool will enable you to think, and that is one of the most important things you can do in a fight. If you don't think, you'll wind up hurt or dead.

Think

Man has the ability to use his mind in a variety of ways. This thinking is what separates us from the other beings on the planet. In the *Tarzan* books I read as a youth, it was Tarzan's mind that set him apart from the other creatures of the jungle.

149

Contrary to what many people might think, fighting is not a stupid man's sport. Yes, I've said fighting is stupid, and it is in most situations. But to actually fight, a person needs to be sharp and quick-thinking if he's going to be good. If this book does anything at all, it should get you thinking about some things.

In the training chapter, I stress the importance of thinking while training so you will do the same in an actual confrontation. I mentioned earlier how Animal said it was good thinking to slam the heavy bag into his face in order to buy me some time to get to the chair in the corner.

You need to always be looking for ways to end the jam once it has started. It's a necessity to be aware of what's going on all around you and be thinking at least two steps ahead of the immediate happenings. Thinking about the consequences of your actions is also a must. Is it life and death, where you need to incapacitate your opponent and flee? (Do you know where you're fleeing?) Or are you working as a bouncer or security guard, where if you hurt the dude you'll be in trouble?

Believe me, when you are in the middle of a brawl, your brain is working in warp drive. It's crucial to take in and evaluate everything. The fortunate thing is that, under these circumstances, many times things seem to slow down. Your senses are so heightened that you take in everything and see more than usual. Many people experience this in accidents. Even though, in actuality, things are happening blindingly fast, you will get this same "slow motion" in many fights.

Visualization, thinking about things beforehand, and thinking during realistic training will increase your ability to think on your feet when you need to. Intellectual games that require quick thinking are also of value. Your mind is like a muscle—the more you use it, the stronger it becomes. And inactivity will result in atrophy of your mental quickness.

I'll pass on some sound advice that I'm sure you've probably heard before: pull your head out and think about what you're doing!

The attitude and determination to never be beat, accompanied by the ability to remain calm and to think during the heat of battle, are far more important than techniques you may learn. Develop the mind-set that Richard Marcinko conveys with his final words in his autobiography, *Rogue Warrior*—"I will not fail"—not only during a fight, but in everything you do.

FAST AND FURIOUS

CHAPTER 15

"He who hesitates

meditates—horizontally!"

—Ed Parker

There's an old saying that there are two kinds of gunfighters: the quick and the dead. (This saying was around way before the Sharon Stone movie.) How true, and it applies to every form of combat out there. I don't care if you are talking about a school-yard fistfight, a fencing match, a knife fight, a gunfight, or a full-scale war between armies. Speed is an absolute necessity in any form of combat.

Way back when, Nabeshima Naoshige told his army of samurai, "When things are done leisurely, seven out of ten turn out poorly. A warrior is one who does things fast." Speed, however, is a component of

153

several aspects of fighting. Speed is of the essence when executing a technique, of course. You don't want to give the guy time to move, block, take a nap, or go to a store and buy a gun to blow you away. But speed is also of importance as to when you launch your techniques or counters. (I believe that the first punch thrown can also be a form of counter. If you know for sure the SOB is going to try and hurt you and you knock him out, that's a counter.) If a guy grabs you, or tries to grab you, you'll have a much better chance of getting out of the situation unscathed if you act immediately, quickly, and with speed. Get the point?

The events that occurred one night in Tong Du Chong illustrate just how quickly things can erupt and why it is important to be one of the fastest and most ferocious in an encounter. John's girlfriend had a friend visiting from Seoul, so the four of us went out for dinner and then to a dance club. We were sitting there with our drinks when two big dudes came in. They were big—the biggest two in the bar—and they were acting the part. They were very loud, obnoxious, pushy, and so forth. The way they were acting, it wasn't hard to know where they were in the bar, and I sort of kept my eye on them. John and Su headed for the dance floor, and since her friend didn't speak much English, we soon followed. Then one of the big two started push his way through the crowd. As he passed by my date, he grabbed her behind, which made her cower a little toward John and me. I immediately shot a hand out and grabbed the guy's arm, and said, "You don't do shit like that."

"Touch me again and I'll pound your ass," he barked, as he pulled his arm free and stared down at me.

I was looking up and thinking of how big this guy was, but undaunted I said, "You won't pound my ass."

Just as these words exited my mouth, his arm shot out and grabbed me by the throat. He was cocking his other hand back

154

to throw an overhand right that probably would have pulverized me. I mean, this guy was huge.

I knew that I didn't want to be on the receiving end of that blow, so I leapt into action, throwing a quick punch to his face and then hitting him with a tackle, giving it everything I had. We both went down to the floor with me on top. As we hit the floor, I started pounding him for all I was worth. There was no way I was going to give him another chance. He had sunglasses on top of his head, and I remember smashing them into his forehead. I repeatedly landed blows to his face and head as he tried to cover up and roll out from under me. He finally managed to turn and cover his face, so I started pounding on his exposed ribs. This whole encounter only lasted a short time, and then a bunch of people who know me started trying to get me to stop. "Burrese, he's had enough," came a chorus of voices. I stopped and got to my feet.

Unbeknownst to me at this time, the guy's big friend had tried to pull me off the guy, but John pulled him away and said, "Stay out—it's one on one." The guy ignored John and started for my back again, so John grabbed him and punched him once.

It was about this time that I stopped pummeling my giant, and people got in the way of John and his. In situations like this, things get pretty chaotic, and John and I and the girls were separated.

Then the guy John had punched came back after him, and the two of them started into it. At the same time, the entire bar erupted. People were fighting all over the place—it was just like the movies. The bouncer grabbed me and said I started it, and he wanted to throw me out or hold me for the police. I wasn't about to be thrown out or held; my buddy was still fighting. I slammed the bouncer to the ground and made my way to where I saw John, while pushing people out of my way and trying to avoid getting hit. I didn't know why most of the people were fighting, I just knew John, the girls, and I needed to get lost before the MPs showed up, which would be soon.

When I got to John, he had just messed giant number two up bad. I yelled that we needed to get the girls and get out of there. We did, and just in time. As we got outside, we saw the MPs. We did some E & E, hiding in some bushes as one group of MPs passed on foot, and we managed to get out of the area without being arrested.

This story shows that everything that is calm and peaceful can change in an instant. Things get fast and furious, and you have to be ready to do the same if you want to come out unscathed. So let's look at some of the principles behind being fast and furious.

SPEED OF TECHNIQUE

The importance of speed when executing a technique can not be overlooked. In his book *Training and Fighting Skills*, Benny "The Jet" Urquidez states that "Speed is the most important overall development for karate competition." It's the same on the street, only more so. You need speed when executing both offensive and defensive techniques.

This means you need to punch, kick, knee, etc. as fast as possible while utilizing quick blocks, ducks, and parries to keep from being hit. Remember, if your opponent is throwing lightning-fast blows at your precious body, you have to be faster than lightning!

Okay, okay, okay—speed's important. How do you get it? Funny you should ask—I have an answer. Part of speed is genetic. It has to do with the amount of fast-twitch and slow-twitch muscle fibers you have. You will find that world-class sprinters like Carl Lewis will have a greater ratio of fast-twitch fibers, and champion marathon runners have a greater ratio of slow-twitch fibers. Sorry, there's nothing you can do about the ratio you are fixed with. You can improve what you have, though. This is done by practicing. Good old repetition!

Repetition, the mother of all learning, is the single most important ingredient in increasing your speed. As you repeat the technique over and over, your muscles become accustomed to the motion. It becomes easier, and you become faster. As you train, the action will become a reflex. You develop these reflexes through hours of repetition training. When you have stepped off to the side and blocked a punch coming at you in practice thousands of times, it will come instinctively to you in a hostile situation. Your reflexes will take over and handle the confrontation when you are surprised. So when you first start training, you must mentally concentrate on the action you want your body to perform. Block, punch, get out of the way, etc. But after you've practiced long enough, the moves just sort of flow and you don't have to really think about them anymore. You just do them. That is what you want, and that is what you should train for.

The key to speed besides having it down pat from lots of repetition is to relax. You can throw a much faster punch or kick when you are relaxed. You don't want to be all tensed up while executing any technique. Relax and let your body flow. You should be able to snake your blow out to your opponent with your body relaxed until the time of contact. This is easiest to practice with punches. Get a heavy bag and throw some basic jabs. Keep your arm relaxed right up to the point of contact. Mess around with this and see how it feels. Once you discover the feel of the movement, you'll understand it a lot better. (Doing something always remains with you better than just reading or watching it.)

Then start experimenting with increasing your speed on other techniques. Remember, you need to have the technique down to where you don't think about it, and then work on making it faster. This will not only ensure that your blocks and parries save you from being hit and that your strikes land, but speed is also one of those key ingredients to power, remember? So you'll be super quick and more powerful to boot.

Having lightning-fast techniques will be of little good if you don't have a chance to use them. Or if you fail to use them when you have a chance. Quite often this will be the case when dealing with a sucker puncher. If you aren't paying attention, he'll clobber you before you know what the hell's going on. (There's that awareness bit again. It sure must be important.) Then there are those who recognize the threat, and may see it coming, but fail to react and counter before they get creamed. So let's look at the other areas where speed is of the essence.

YOU SNOOZE YOU LOSE

I really like General George S. Patton, Jr. He was a great leader on the battlefield, and I agree with many of his philosophies of combat, one of which was his belief in speed. He would tell his troops that they should keep moving fast. He didn't believe in stopping to dig in; he just kept going. "Grab 'em by the nose and kick 'em in the pants," he would tell them. "You keep movin' and you will never be in the enemy's gun sight" (Porter B. Williamson, *Patton's Principles*).

Before every action, you must first make a decision. In a combat situation, whether a war or a schoolyard fistfight, that action based on your decision must come about quickly. Once you determine that someone is intending to do you bodily harm, you must react instantly. You don't have time to lollygag around; you need to act. That's why it's important to be aware and realize the threat as early as possible. This gives you a little extra time. Hopefully, you'll recognize stuff early enough to avoid the entire confrontation rather than resort to the reflexes you have honed through consistent, realistic repetition.

158

So you see, you can become faster just by being more aware. One element that determines how fast you are is your reaction time. That's what I meant when I said you could have quick techniques but not use them. As I said, before you do any move or counter, you must first decide to do it. The time it takes you to recognize you need to do something, decide what to do, and then do it is your reaction time.

Two things can improve your reaction time. The first is being aware of what's happening. The sooner you recognize a threat, the more time you have to react. This extra time, in a sense, is making you faster. It's like giving yourself a head start in a race. You might not be running faster, but you make it to the finish line first because of the headstart. I don't know about you, but I'll take any headstart I can get when it means my survival is on the line. There is no "fair play" in a fight.

The second way reaction time is increased is in making the decision to do something and determining what it is you need to do faster. The best way to make sure you make quick, accurate decisions is to make them beforehand. You do this by training. If you have trained and have those moves down pat, you'll instinctively react and your reflexes will take over. That's what reflexes are. Your body is making the decision and acting before your conscious thought can. For this reason, it is good to be very proficient at a few techniques rather than being mediocre at many. If you don't have some basics down, you will stop and think about what you should do. While you are thinking, you're going to get nailed.

My dad remembers a time in Kansas when he and another guy were out on the town having a little fun. My dad was off to the side when a guy came up with a knife. He was looking for a quick score on a couple of GIs. (Soldiers always have money, right?) He made a move toward the guy my dad was with, and before you could really see what was going on, my dad's companion had the knife swung around and the attacker's stomach sliced wide open, with intestines spilled out and blood covering the area.

Dad's companion that night had had a lot of formal training in combative arts as well as real-life confrontations. He just instinctively reacted when the knife was drawn. There was no thought involved at all. It was an immediate threat to his life, for he had no doubt that the guy would stick him if he got the chance. His training kicked in, and he did what had to be done. Sure, some will say he overreacted; he didn't have to lay the guy's guts open. Maybe that's true, and maybe he did know other techniques that would have stopped the altercation in a different manner. The thing is, he really didn't think about it. He just did it. That's what happens when someone who is well trained gets into a fight. That's the level you want to be at if you are attacked. No thinking, just action. In Japanese, there's a word, *mushin*. It means, no-mindedness, or without thought. The samurai strived to enter this psychological state during battle. They would let nothing interpose the impulse to action and the action itself.

Before any of this can happen, you must have the right mental attitude. You must realize that in an encounter, speed is of the essence. You must react. Even if what you do isn't the best thing, it's probably better than nothing. The key is to do something, anything—just react. *Don't be a victim!*

When that big SOB grabbed me by the throat and started to wind up his arm to pummel me, I didn't really know what to do. I didn't do any fancy stuff like you see in the movies, either. The main thing was that I didn't stand there and let the guy hit me. He was too big to mess with. So I did what came to mind at the moment: I tackled him and started pounding him for all I was worth. As soon as I had the upper hand, I wasn't going to give him a second chance. I wanted to end it fast, before he had a chance to do any damage to me.

What saved me that night was the fact that I launched into him immediately. I reacted with everything I had. We are right back to the old infantry principles. My reaction surprised him. Speed will be on your side when surprising someone. They don't expect you to fight back, and when you do quickly, it catches them off guard. Surprise is a key, and speed of action is a way to get that surprise.

So train hard and learn your techniques so that they are instinctive. Relax while executing them. Be aware of what's going on to improve your reaction time. Give yourself that head start. Have the attitude that you will react immediately, and don't hesitate when the time comes; do something. Go to the left or go to the right, but don't stand in the middle. If you do, you'll get squashed. And remember Yamamoto Tsunetomo's words in *Hagakure: The Book of the Samurai:* "The way of the samurai is immediacy."

FRIENDS YOU RUN WITH

CHAPTER 16

"Greater love hath no man than this, that

a man lay down his life for his friends."

—New Testament

John 15:13

Throughout this book I've been mentioning friends and situations we've gotten ourselves into and out of. Sure, there are times when trouble starts and you are all alone. Sometimes you may even be out looking for it by yourself. But unless you are very reclusive, you probably spend a large part of the time with other people. Who you are with when a confrontation develops can be a decisive factor in the outcome.

When trouble erupts, it's crucial that you know how the people you are with will respond. Will they be there beside you till the end, or will they be miles away when you are counting on them? If you don't know, never assume anything!

I knew a guy at Bragg who learned this the hard way for sure. He was a cherry (a new guy), and he was still hanging out with a couple of guys he met at the in-processing station. (It's pretty common when you arrive at a new post to hang out with the first guys you meet until you get to know the guys in your own company.) This guy was down at the Fayetteville Burger King one night when some trouble started. I don't know all of the details, but I do know that a couple of the guys he was with bugged out on him and left him hanging, and that a crowbar to the face ended his military career before it even got started.

He was in the hospital for a long time, and when he got out he had a medical profile for even longer. He couldn't jump again because of all of the tubes in his sinuses, and when you can't jump, you're not very useful in an airborne unit. I think he ended up getting out of the army entirely with a medical discharge.

I can't say for certain that if he had been with different people he wouldn't have been messed up so bad, but I sure as hell think so.

Who you run with makes a big difference in how things turn out when the situation gets ugly, and it deserves some thought. Again, I'm not going to lay down any strict rules. It's up to you what you do and with whom. I'm just giving you a few more things to think about.

As I mentioned above, an important consideration is whether your buddies will be around when things go sour. The majority of my friends, and all of the people I call "true friends," are people I can trust to back me in any situation. They know that I would always be there to back them also.

I remember a time when John came back from Seoul, Korea, and told me he wished I had been with him: "If you would have been there we could have taken them." John and two other guys he was with had gotten themselves into a little trouble with five or six Koreans in a bar that weekend. As John prepared to throw down, he looked for the other two and found that they had exited at warp speed at the sign of a fight. At the same time he realized this: one of the Koreans kicked him in the face a couple of times. Yes, two times! John said the guy's kicks were quicker than lightning, but they didn't have much power behind them.

Now, John was a lot like me in the area of being threatened and throwing down at the drop of a hat. Like me, he also didn't like anyone getting in any licks without him getting some in back. So, as he was getting kicked and realizing he was on his own with a circle of Koreans closing in, he opted to get the hell out of there. Yes, if I'd been there things would have gone down differently. Sure, we may have ended up in jail, but I sort of doubt it. We were both pretty good at E and E, too.

John and I knew that the other would always be there if needed. It was John who stepped in and helped the night we took on the two giants. John didn't even know what it was about. He knew I was fighting and a third party was entering against me. So he joined in to keep things even, no questions asked.

This kind of trust is important. If you know the person or people you are with, it gives you a sense of security. It also enables you to play "hero" once in a while, which I used to do quite regularly.

One such occasion was at a bar/restaurant that we used to frequent in Fayetteville. I was out with Jeff and Darin, and we were just wanting a relaxing evening.

This place happened to have a waiter who was a homosexual. I don't care what your feelings toward homosexuals are, but this guy always treated us very well and we liked

165

him. Hell, he always filled us in on the good looking, unescorted women in the place.

We were sitting at the bar that evening, and three other GIs were sitting at the bar around the corner from us. Where they were sitting, the waiters and waitresses had to pass right behind them going to and from the kitchen. When our waiter would pass by them, they would make comments or grab for his ass. I noticed this a couple of times and saw that it was becoming upsetting for our waiter friend.

"That needs to stop," I said to Jeff and Darin as I stood up.

"What?" they asked.

"Those guys are giving Joey a bad time," I answered. I then casually walked behind the three. Of course they ignored me and had no idea what I was up to. So I turned and walked back over to them. "Why didn't you grab for my ass when I walked by?"

"Hey, we know Joey. So don't worry about it. It's none of your business." The main instigator said to me.

"I know Joey too, and it's bothering him. I'm making it my business, and I want the three of you to leave." I answered calmly.

"And who's going to make us?" came the reply that I was expecting.

"I will," I answered, "and if needed, those two over there will help." They looked over to where I motioned and saw Jeff and Darin smiling. Both of them waved. I walked back over and sat down. Within two minutes, the three finished their drinks, paid their bill, and left. A few minutes after that, the manager came out and thanked us for what we did. He said he had witnessed the happenings also, and was about to ask them to leave when I beat him to it. I told him it was no problem.

The point to this is that I couldn't have done that if I didn't know that Jeff and Darin would back me. Sure, nothing happened in that incident. But it could have, and that's when you'd better know the people you are with.

I did the same kind of thing countless times in Korea. Frank, Brian, and I hated jerks who acted up in the bars we played pool in. So I often asked people to leave. Many times they listened, but if they wanted it to get physical, so be it. I always knew that Frank and Brian would be there, and there wasn't much that we couldn't handle. I talk more about these times in Korea in the chapter on drunks.

Elsewhere, I mentioned the importance of having witnesses in certain circumstances. Having a friend to back your story can keep you out of trouble after the damage has been done. Sometimes, however, having the right friend around can keep you out of trouble in the first place.

Many of my friends and I had a general rule that we would mind our own business if it was a one-on-one that didn't pertain to us. But at times, it was much more appropriate to step in and stop things rather than let the situation play out with possible unfortunate consequences. In other words, save your buddy's ass from winding up in a sling.

I don't know what it was about this guy in my platoon at Bragg, but he sure got on people's nerves. I remember one night when Mark came running to my room, shouting, "Alain, you need to come and stop Jeff. He's going to kill Wood."

I went down there and intervened—not because I cared if Wood got pounded on a bit; I just didn't want Jeff to get into trouble. I ended up having to hold Jeff back while Mark and a couple of others ushered Wood back to his room and told him to stay there. The idiot was running off at the mouth the entire time and I almost let Jeff have him.

As I said, this guy could be irritating. It wasn't long after the above incident when Jeff and a couple others pulled me off of him. He mouthed off at the wrong time. They pulled me away for the same reason—they didn't care that I was punching him; they were just keeping me out of trouble.

That wasn't the only time I was glad to have a friend or two looking out for me. One night in Korea, Frank saved me from a good beating for sure. I was pissed off—probably over a woman or for some other stupid reason; I don't remember for sure. I do remember leaving the bar even madder than when I had entered. I had been sitting there brooding while drinking whiskey and Coke, and I was getting madder by the second. Frank, being a good friend, decided to follow me to see if I was okay.

I've mentioned that I hate bullies, and it really pisses me off when someone starts something with someone smaller. Through this belief, I was looking for a justification to start something. I couldn't just go up to someone and lay into him, or I'd be no better than those I dislike. (Oh, how anger clouds one's thinking.) I decided that starting a fight with six guys wouldn't be bullying; I was way outnumbered. Anger and alcohol contribute to stupidness all the time, and this was no exception.

So, in the middle of the street, in Tokori, South Korea, I was mouthing off to six other GIs. I have no clue as to who they were; I was just looking for someone to take my frustrations out on. Just before a couple of them took me up on my taunts, Frank caught up with me and saw what was about to transpire, mainly my getting stomped.

He did some talking to the group and then forcefully walked me in the opposite direction from where they were heading, telling me what a dumb ass I was. Not only was I trying to start trouble with six guys, but it was in a prime location to get busted by the MPs. And that would amount to a loss of rank and pay. We went down the road and I threw some large rocks into the river and wore myself out trying to get a 400-pound length of cement culvert over my head. I was certain that I could lift it overhead and toss it down into the river with the rocks. Frank still laughs and reminds me of that night.

Anyway, Frank saved me from a beating and possibly getting arrested that night. Those are the kinds of friends to run with. (Of course, if you put them through that kind of incident on a regular basis, they might get tired of bailing you out of trouble, and you'll be looking for someone else to spend time with.) And you are always there for them when they need a hand, helping with trouble or helping them avoid it, whichever comes down the road.

This concept can carry over into jobs that sometimes require getting physical. You need to know how the people you are working with will react to violent encounters.

I had a number of part-time jobs during college, including Resident Assistant, night security for a dorm, and concert security for different shows that performed on our campus. I talk more on these and other jobs in the chapter, "Sometimes You Have To." What is important here is knowing the people you are working with.

My friend Dave held the same jobs when he was in college. (Actually, he's the one who helped me get hired on in all three.) At one concert, he and another guy went into a crowd to break up a fight. They thought the other security personnel were right behind them, but as it turned out, the others held back. That's what happens sometimes when you have untrained people in certain positions. Anyway, it was a lot tougher for Dave and the other security person, Alex, to break the stuff up by themselves than it would have been with six of them. They were lucky. They were risking personal injury when they didn't need to. If they had known that the others were going to hold back, they would have called over somebody else or given them direct instructions to follow. The only real good thing about this was that the guy Dave went into the crowd with was one of the security supervisors. Dave was always hired back to work any concert he wanted, and the others didn't work again.

One of the reasons Alex and Dave were able to handle the situation alone was their attitude. Even though they were in a potentially dangerous situation and outnumbered, they kept their cool and took charge of the ordeal. They were in uniform and just acted like they were in control. Often this is enough to control a crowd. If you back down, or show a lack of control, you will lose a crowd. Once you've lost it, it's super tough to regain control, and people start getting hurt.

I've mentioned that we used to have a code of honor that if it was a one-on-one we'd stay out of it. Not always! Again, different situations call for different reactions. When you are working, you are always a team. If you want to go it alone and ask your buddies to stay out of it on the street, fine. But not on the job.

One night Dave and I were working together at the dorm. I was the Resident Assistant on duty and he was the night security. A couple were outside the front door, and the guy was yelling furiously at his girlfriend. Dave and I headed outside, with him going out the door first, "Is there a problem here?" he asked.

"Yeah, there's a fucking problem!" the guy yelled as he punched Dave in the mouth. Neither of us expected the guy to start throwing punches at us. I immediately went for my old favorite—the half throw, half drag down that ends with me on top. There was no, "This is Dave's fight"—we were working together.

Dave recovered from the punch almost immediately and was only a half-second behind me. So as I was taking the guy around the neck for my takedown, Dave hit the guy low, and he went down with the two of us on top of him. He was struggling for all he was worth, but with my arm tightening around his neck and Dave keeping the rest of him immobilized, he wasn't going anywhere.

We held him there, listening to him threatening to pound us, while a third party called the campus police. We turned him over and then filled out the necessary reports.

It was so funny—as the cops were being filled in on what had happened, the guy told me that when he was in the army they settled things by fighting and said I was a pussy for calling the cops. I told him that if we were back in the army I would have slammed his head against the sidewalk a few times and left. That way I wouldn't be spending the night filing a report.[1]

The point is, when you know and trust the people you are with, you know when to fight, when to watch, and when to keep each other out of trouble. Who you're with is important, so don't take it lightly.

The last little tale I'll use to illustrate the importance of this involves my buddy Greg. One night he was out roaming the streets in South Korea when a guy came up and started some trouble with him. That would have been okay, but another guy came out of the blue and all Greg remembers is coming to and having this guy he'd never seen before kicking him in the ribs. The thing is, he was with two other people. They just sat and watched, even when he was unconscious and being kicked. To make matters worse, on different occasions Greg got two different reports on what happened. So he still doesn't really know what actually happened that night.

Same guy, Greg, different night, different friends down in the same town in Korea. This time Greg was down there with a couple good friends he could trust. Trouble started, and before he knew it, Greg was on the bottom of a pile of four guys trying to pummel him through the floor. Luckily, they were getting in each other's way and he wasn't receiving many serious blows. Greg says, "I was just sitting there under those guys, and I was as calm as could be. I knew any second that Clark and Mayo would be pulling them off me. And sure

171

enough, in a couple seconds they were flying off. I saved the last for me and beat him into the floor."

I've had people tell me that I'd be their first pick to have with them, whether in a bar fight or if we had to go to actual combat. I have a small group that I feel the same about. Whatever you're doing, get to know the people you run with. They can and will make a difference.

NOTES

1. Remember what I said in the chapter on going to the ground about smashing a guy's head into the pavement? It's serious, and you run the risk of spending time in a jail cell or a courtroom rather than just filing a report. Remember to think about these things.

WOMEN

CHAPTER 17

"Now, Watson, the fair sex

is your department."

—Sherlock Holmes

The Second Stain

If you are hoping that I'm going to give you some tremendous insight into understanding women, I'm sorry, but I haven't figured them out myself yet. I am going to disclose some experiences and advice on how to deal with situations that often involve women, though. Things like getting into trouble because you are upset over a woman, not being aware because you're flirting around, and what to do when you're with a woman when a crisis starts.

If you are a male reading this, you'll probably relate to a lot of it. If you are a woman reading this, it's not meant to be insulting. You may learn a little about how

173

we men think, and it will help you figure us out some. I sort of doubt it, though. Men and women have been trying to figure one another out for an enormous length of time, and we still can't do it.

First, let's discuss the trouble caused by women. That sounds good and is what we like to believe, but actually, guys, most of it is caused by how we react to the situation that the woman is involved in.

Sure, I was mad. Wouldn't you be upset if some girl was using you to make her boyfriend jealous, and as soon as he was, she told you to kiss off? The boyfriend had thought of saying or doing something to me, but his brother, who worked with me in a sawmill at the time, told him it wouldn't be a very good idea.

So there I was, out in the parking lot, venting my frustrations to a couple of buddies, when some half-drunk squid doing cookies in the parking lot slammed into my parked truck. I swear it wasn't more than two minutes earlier that I had told my friends, "That asshole better be careful—my truck's over there."

Before the sound of the crash faded, I was heading over to his car. I vaguely heard Matt say, "He'll kill him." Remember, I was already upset and it didn't take much more to really set me off. As I got to his car, he opened the door and started to get out. I punched him in the mouth and it sat him back into the seat. I was livid. In situations like this, getting into a physical confrontation is like fanning a fire. I was getting madder by the second and I was sort of pacing back and forth by the car. He stood up and took a step toward me while he started to say something. I didn't listen or give him a second; I hit him again. It was with an open hand this time, but right on the chin. He went down on his ass and lay there looking at the sky. My friends ran over to stop me from doing anything else to him, while one of his friends started saying shit to me. I

174

started challenging him and his cronies (remember, I was steaming at this point). No one else would take me on, and I started to calm down with the help of my buddy's mom, who had been down at the bar with us.

Anyway, to wrap this up, I was cited with misdemeanor assault and had to pay a fine and keep myself out of trouble for the next six months. The guy who hit my truck was ordered by the court to pay for the damages, but he went back to the navy and decided he wouldn't pay. (He was home on leave when the incident happened, and I didn't feel as bad when I learned he was a squid. Sorry, navy guys, but you understand.) I gave him several months and listened to all of his excuses before I finally got fed up and called his XO. I was in the military too, so I knew how to play the game. The military frowns on soldiers not paying their debts, so the day after I talked to his XO he called me and had his mother pay me in full. Even with my comment above, I have to say that the navy chain of command took care of the situation very quickly, and I called his XO back and told him thanks and that the money had been paid.

One last interesting note: when I was talking to his mother to tell her the exact amount to write the check for and where to send it, she told me that I was just lucky his brothers hadn't been there. There was that threat thing that I have such a problem with again. I told her that they were lucky and she responded, "I don't think so, there are three of them."

Naturally, I told her, "Then all three of them would have been on their asses." She slammed the phone down on me. I guess some people have trouble accepting reality.

Let's get back to the purpose of this story. If I wouldn't have been upset over the girl in the bar, I probably wouldn't have rushed over and punched the guy in the mouth. That would have saved me a trip to the judge, and I could have used the money I paid on the fine for something I wanted rather than supporting the town I was visiting that night.

175

Sometimes there's nothing like dishing out cold hard cash that you've worked for to make you realize how stupid your actions were. Unfortunately, it has taken me more than once to learn this lesson. I have hit people, ripped off doors, punched cars (cost me over $300 for punching a car once), and a whole lot of other stupid shit because of being upset over a woman or two, as the case may have been. It's not worth it! Again, it's not the women; it's how you react to the situations. You don't have to react violently. You don't have to get yourself into trouble.

I have learned that I have the greatest difficulties in controlling myself when I am dealing with emotions over a woman. It's not necessarily women, but my emotional attachment to them. Often, it has been the pain caused by rejection or loss that has set me off. I can deal with physical pain from a punch or a kick a lot easier than I deal with the emotional trauma of mixed up or hurt feelings. I realize this now and have taken steps to get this part of my life under control. If you find that you are in the same detrimental circle, take some time to pinpoint just why and what you are doing. Get control over yourself now rather than doing something that will cost you a lot of money, or worse. Many people who have been unable to control themselves when experiencing feelings of pain and rejection from a failed relationship or whatever have ended up turning to violence and landed themselves in prison or the morgue. *It's not worth it!*

When no emotional attachment is involved, it is fairly easy to ignore women and not become upset with their actions. This proves that it isn't the woman as much as how you are reacting to the circumstances. Rhett and I got into an argument one night in a bar in Fayetteville with two women. Our buddy, Todd, was trying to pick up their friend, and we were patiently waiting on him while the discussion with the other two turned sour. The two women started in on Rhett and I on how women jumped out of planes also and were going on in this direction. I was getting annoyed at the whole discussion and just wanted to leave. So I said something rather sexist and racist, and the one went crazy. She started hitting, kicking, scratching, and generally trying her damnedest to do bodily harm to my body.

Now, before I get labeled as a politically incorrect white supremacist, let me explain what I said. Yes, it's true that women also jump out of planes. But Rhett, Todd, and I were all airborne infantry, which doesn't include women. So we just pointed out that women don't march 15 miles with a 60-pound or heavier ruck after they hit the ground like we did.

At this time, I was interested in a Japanese girl who was going to college back in Montana. This will explain my next comment. Remember, I was becoming very annoyed at the whole situation, so I told the two, "Look, men are better than women and Japanese women are better than white women."

That's when all hell broke loose. And some people say only men have tempers and get violent. As I said, she was coming at me with everything she had.

I was always raised to never hit a woman under any circumstances. The reasoning is pretty clear. If I can put a 250-pound man into the hospital, what would happen if I started punching a 130-pound woman? Well, in this incident I almost lost it. I was doing pretty well and was just keeping her from doing any real damage to me. Fingernails can give a person some nasty scratches, whether from a woman or a man, especially to the eyes.

As I was keeping her hands away from my face, I was actually a little amused by the whole ordeal, and luckily the annoyance wasn't anything worse—that is, until the hot coffee hit me in the face and chest. Her friend had come back with a cup of it and splashed it all over me. I'm glad to this day that it was only hot enough to hurt and turn my skin red and not hot enough to give me serious burns. It did hurt some, though, and Rhett said that for a moment I got "that look" in my eyes and he thought I was going to go off. I didn't, and some guy who was a friend of the women came over and said, "Don't you hit her." He didn't say it very forcefully, which is lucky for him, because I did consider smacking him just because I couldn't hit the women. Actually, the women would have probably given me a better fight than he would have, so I just pushed her to him and walked out of the place with Rhett, muttering how crazy some women were. Rhett commended me on my self-control, especially after the coffee, and we waited outside for Todd, who had missed the whole ordeal.

So you see, if I can control myself not to hit a woman, even when it's a woman I'm mad at, I can control myself not to go looking for trouble and hitting some guy when I'm mad at a woman.

Animal talks a little about this in a video he did with Peyton Quinn and Mike Haynack (*Barroom Brawling: The Art of Staying Alive in Beer Joints, Biker Bars, and Other Fun Places*). He talks about most fights being over a guy's ego. Who controls your ego? You do!

Remember what old Lao-Tsu said in *Tao Teh King*: "He who knows much about others may be learned, but he who understands himself is more intelligent. He who controls others may be powerful, but he who has mastered himself is mightier still." If you are like I was (and still am to a certain degree) and turn to physical violence when you're upset over a woman, learn this about yourself and look for alternate ways to manage your feelings. If you don't, sooner or later you'll find yourself in more trouble than you can get yourself out of. I talk more about ways to do this in the chapter on realizing when you don't have to fight.

On a different note, remember the one half of the old awareness definition? It's also being aware of how your actions affect the situation. Since that incident long ago in Fayetteville, I've done a lot of studying on communication. The comments I made were, to say the least, inappropriate. I now know how to handle situations much more gracefully and tactfully. It's a skill I would encourage everyone to work on. Not only does it make life much easier without as many confrontations, it can keep you from getting your eyes scratched out by some crazy woman in a bar some night.

That's enough about when you are upset over women. What about when everything is going great with the girl you're with? You and she are just strolling along with your heads in the clouds and not a trouble in the world. Pretty picture, right? Well, it is! But it doesn't mean you can let your guard down completely and forget all about being aware of your surroundings.

Again, this advice is coming from firsthand experience. At times, I'm one of the most aware people around, and many of my friends were quite surprised that this happened to me. But it did, so I'll tell you about it here.

I was on my way to a restaurant in Saigon with the friends I was touring with. There was romantic interest between me and one of my companions, and we were spending a great deal of time flirting. I was concentrating on her rather than on other things going on.

Now, before I lay all the blame on my concentrating on my female companion, I must also add that I had spent the last couple of days a little farther north in Ca Na and Phan Rang, seeing some of the places my dad spent time in during the war. Besides my father being a vet, I've known many others and have read many accounts on Vietnam. So I know all about the things that went on with the Vietnamese kids. But all of the kids I ran into up in Phan Rang were really innocent, and a lot of them are pretty cute. Now, I'm sure there are those out there who would say no one is really innocent, but the fact is,

I didn't have any trouble and found the people to be genuinely friendly and trustworthy.

But back in Saigon it was a different story. Just as everywhere else in the world, city kids are a little different. So there I was, surrounded by a group of cute kids wanting to sell me postcards. (These postcard kids are all over the place there.) The kids were cute, and I was flirting with Marilyn as we headed for the restaurant to have a nice dinner. Everything was great, and I didn't have a care in the world. Not until later that is, when I realized that they had lifted my wallet. I lost $300, a Visa card, my Japanese ID, and my Japanese bank cash card. It could have been a lot worse; at least I had friends to loan me money until we got back to Japan.

The money was nothing compared to the anger I felt at myself. I mean, me—"Mr. Awareness"—having his wallet stolen! I've written and talked about being aware. I stressed the importance of being aware to the girls before and during the trip to Vietnam. And now it was me who was ripped off. Talk about feeling stupid! Remember what I've said about knowing something but still messing up? Everything I know—and usually instinctively do—was thrown to the wind that evening, and I was shown that it doesn't really matter what you know if you don't use it.

So, just what are the main points to this? First, you can be aware 95 percent of the time and lose it all if you pick the wrong 5 percent to put your guard down. Don't ever be so distracted by one thing that you miss other important things happening. You could be giving your complete attention to some hostile-looking character down the street and miss his companion coming up to blindside you. Or, like me, you could be concentrating on something positive and forget to be keeping an eye out for suspicious or dangerous happenings.

Second, not everything is as it appears. This is rather obvious, but people forget it all the time. Those cute, friendly kids lifted my wallet. There are a lot of con artists out there, and every person who has been taken will say, "He didn't seem like the type that would do that. He seemed so nice," and so on. I'm not advocating that we all turn into paranoid, cynical, distrusting souls. It just pays to be careful. I still bought more postcards from kids in Vietnam. Not all of them are out to steal from you. But you can bet that I was a little more aware of what they were doing around me from then on.

Third, no one is invincible. I've said this earlier and I'll repeat it here. Even though I know all this stuff, I failed to use it when it counted. Maybe this was a good lesson for me: I should practice what I preach. Yes, people were surprised that it happened to me, and I was mad at myself for letting it happen. But it may have been partially due to my "it can't happen to me" attitude. Hey, it *can* happen to me, and I need to keep my eyes open just like everyone else. So, before you go out and let something happen to you because you aren't paying attention and you don't think it will happen to you, remember this tale and keep yourself out of trouble.

So now you're out with your significant other and you're paying attention to what's going on and trouble starts brewing. What do you do? Well, there are as many different answers as there are situations you may find yourself in. However, here are a few things to think about.

I personally feel that my main objective in any situation is to ensure the safety of the person I'm with and then myself. The surest way to accomplish this is to get her and myself away from the situation altogether. If this means I have to turn tail and run too, so be it. Her safety is most important. Any physical encounter will be a last-ditch effort because everything else failed.

The classic "Run baby, I'll hold them off" isn't practical. For one, most women won't run off and leave the man they care about alone. Just as you care about her, she cares about you. Second, where and what is she running to? Stick together and get both of you out of the situation.

Again, different situations will warrant different actions, and at times things happen so fast that you have to go physical without thinking. There are no exact rules, just things to think about beforehand so you'll be a little better prepared to react if you have to. At times it will depend on the woman you are with as well as the situation.

The time John and I sent those two giants to the hospital was traumatizing to his girlfriend. She bawled for a long time and kept crying about how much blood there was. She wasn't that reassured by John's saying, "Hey, it wasn't our blood!" Her friend, the one who was grabbed, was also very scared and shaken up by the ordeal.

So what you do should be based on both the situation and who you are with. My friend Dave was at a bar with his girlfriend one night, and when they went outside, trouble was brewing. Dave quickly ushered her away, and they left the area. If it would have been me with Dave, rather than his girlfriend, we might have at least looked into what was going on. As it turned out, the paper the next morning told the story. A guy was killed in the fight that went on that Dave avoided. Dave did the best thing possible. Neither he nor his girlfriend was hurt, neither was entangled in the police investigation of the killing, and neither had to see the man who was killed. It is not pleasant seeing a person who has been killed or hurt, and I definitely don't want an enjoyable evening spoiled by witnessing an act of violence that could have been avoided. Besides, talking to the police is a surefire way to miss your dinner reservations.

I'm sorry if I didn't lay out exactly what you should do in each situation. It's sort of like the rules in a street fight—there aren't any! What I've tried to do here is share a couple of my experiences involving women to illustrate that it is something you should think a bit about. Only you know yourself and the women you are with. And only you will be able to assess the situations you are in. Some consideration beforehand will aid you in making crucial decisions during critical times.

One last little note before I quit talking about women. It seems that the lessons about women are the ones that are the least likely to sink in. Guys keep getting into the same trouble over and over again, even when they "know" better. Making mistakes—learning the "hard way"—isn't stupid, but failing to learn from these mistakes is. Dealings with women also seem to be learned best when you go through it yourself. So take my advice and do a little thinking beforehand—about you, your situations, and the women or woman you spend your time with.

WHAT YOU'RE WEARING

CHAPTER 18

"The bigger they are, the longer

you stay unconscious."

—George Carlin

Something many people never discuss or think about is what is worn during a fight. Many times what you have on—or don't have on—can determine who the victor will be. Just as an amateur or professional fighter enters the ring with the proper gear, a person should think about his attire on the street.

I realize that at times you must wear certain dress for the occasion. No one goes out looking for a fight in a suit. However, there are times when getting into a fight is more likely and a few precautions could be beneficial.

A big one involves the wearing of jewelry, including watches. Personally, I have

185

never been one to wear much other than a cheap watch, and at times I have worn something around my neck. Notice that I said cheap watches. This is because it took me a while to learn to take the things off when I was in a place where trouble might start. Thus, I have replaced many watches after losing them or having them broken during some encounter.

There are two things you can do if you wear a watch. One, you can get one of the military commando-style watch bands. They are heavy duty and have a flap that covers and protects the face of the watch. These bands do not break easily, so they usually won't come off in a fight. And the flap protects the watch from damage (as well as preventing it from reflecting light during tactical operations). The other alternative is to take it off when you are in a situation that may escalate into a physical encounter. I rarely enter a bar anymore without taking my watch off and putting it into my pocket. Of course, the latter is not always practical or effective. You may not have time or you may forget to take it off. In this case, I hope you wear cheap ones like I do.[1]

If you wear anything around your neck, there is a good chance it will get broken in a fight. This is good, because if you wear something like I used to sometimes wear made of 550 cord or parachute cord, it could be used against you. Your opponent has enough going for him; you don't need to supply him with something to strangle you with too. As for the chain, or whatever, that gets broken, well that's better than getting choked by it, but I hope it wasn't a gift from someone special. Lesson: don't wear it where trouble might start, or avoid the trouble.

Pierced ears, noses, and other body parts are a person's choice. I personally don't have anything pierced and don't intend to ever have anything pierced. However, I do have friends that wear earrings and such. My advice is don't. But if you insist, wear earrings that are very small. The bigger they are, the easier they are to get a hold of and rip out. It doesn't take much to rip out an earring or nose ring, and it is something that a little planning can prevent.

Rings are something I have never worn, but again, I have friends who wear them. Rings can be good and bad in a fight. They can really mess up the other guy when you punch him. Depending on the ring, they can inflict a lot of damage. My buddy John was wearing a ring in a fight in Korea, and he laid his opponent's face open just above the eye. The guy needed a number of stitches to close it up. At the same time his opponent was at the hospital getting sewn up, however, I was splinting John's broken finger with a chopstick I snapped in half and an elastic band from his girlfriend's hair. You can break your hand easily enough without a ring when you punch something, so I advise against wearing anything on your hands, except maybe a pair of leather gloves that would offer some protection rather than complicate matters. Again, if a conflict looks imminent, slip your rings, watches, and so on into your pocket.

We know footwork is extremely important when it comes to fighting, but the footwear you have on is also important. Remember the old *Billy Jack* movies? He'd take his shoes off before he started to kick people in the teeth. That never made sense to me. Why did he remove his shoes? I've been kicked with bare feet, tennis shoes, and boots, and I'll tell you, the boots hurt the most. I'd much rather be kicked by someone who is barefoot or wearing soft shoes (that is, if I have to be kicked). Chuck Norris' kicks are only made worse by those cowboy boots he wears.

I like cowboy boots, and growing up in Montana I wore them a lot and still do. A cowboy boot can do a lot of damage, as can a biker's boot. I once saw a guy get his head kicked in by another guy with big boots because the first guy messed with the dude's Harley. There's a lesson there that should be rather obvious: *never* mess with anyone's bike. Back to boots—don't start wearing them just to make your kicks worse, because they can hinder a person also. I can run pretty well in boots, but I can run even faster in shoes made for running.

Living in Montana, I also learned to navigate on ice while wearing cowboy boots. If you get into a fight on an icy street wearing cowboy boots, you are not going to be floating around like old Muhammed Ali. You're probably going to end up on the ice real quick, so my philosophy was to take the fight to the ground as quickly as possible. That way, I was at least in control of how we went down. Actually, it doesn't really matter what you're wearing on ice. The best bet is to take the guy down and control him on the ground.

So, what does one wear? Wear what you always wear, if that's what you are comfortable with. Just be aware of the strengths and weaknesses of what you have chosen. Remember, a lot of this book is just to get you thinking about things that you may not have thought about before.

One suggestion—make sure that your shoes or boots won't come off in the middle of the encounter or, worse yet, when you're trying to get away. Try running down an alley with only one shoe sometime and you'll see what I mean. I used to hate Asia for this. I'd always have my shoes tied loose when I was going in and out of places that required you to remove your footwear at the door. Then I'd have to retie them when I went out to the bars. I like to have them tied tight if I'm in a fight or have to run.

As for clothes, naturally something that you can move in is preferred over tight, constricting clothing. I prefer jeans, as long as they aren't too tight, and a loose, comfortable shirt. More than likely your clothes are going to get ripped and ruined. Shirts and jackets get ripped more often than jeans. That's just one of the lesser prices you have to pay.

There was one night when I didn't pay attention to any of these rules. As I've said before, many times you know stuff but forget or ignore it when it could do you the most good. So there I was, standing in my underwear, another broken watch on the ground, and mad as hell because I didn't get to smash the guy who had just been kicking me in the head.

Here's what happened. I was sitting in the living room of my apartment in a bad mood, when I heard two drunks outside. They were yelling and throwing stuff around because the girls who lived above me had asked them to leave. Obviously, these guys had mistakenly thought they were going to get lucky, and they were pissed because they didn't. It wasn't too hard to figure this out by the profanities they were directing upstairs. I decided to go outside. I had a reason—my truck was parked out there and I didn't want anything to happen to it. (Well, that's how I rationalized my going out there.) I was in a foul mood and looking for some action. I'll talk more about this in a later chapter.

Did I expect trouble? Yes! Did I prepare for it? No! I had been sitting there watching TV in a cheap pair of sweat pants and a t-shirt. So I slipped on my shoes, tied them tight, and grabbed a jacket on the way out the door. My watch was still on my wrist as I walked out to the parking lot where they were brooding over and cussing at the girls.

"You looking for a fight?" the shorter but huskier one of the two asked as they noticed me.

"Na, I just don't want anything to happen to my truck," I replied, actually wanting something to go down.

"Well, I'm going to kick your ass!" he barked as he started toward me. I just stood there with my hands in my jacket pockets, deciding whether I should use the keychain I had that could be used as a nasty weapon. It was too late to grab the ax handle I had in my truck. What the hell—there were only two of them.

As he approached, he was stating how he was going to stomp me in rather colorful terms. As he neared me, I decided against using the keychain and took the fight to him. I hit him first with a quick right to the jaw and then used my old favorite judo throw/takedown. I grabbed him around the head and dragged/threw him to the ground with me on top. As we landed, I started pounding his head and face with hammer fists with my left hand. My right arm was still around his neck, holding him in place to wail on him.

This was working great until his friend, who I wasn't thinking of, came up from behind and started kicking me in the back of the head. Luckily, he was only wearing tennis shoes, and I scrunched up my neck and took most of the kicks on the back and shoulders. (Remember what I said about shoes versus boots? Another thing—he could have done more damage if he would have stomped on me rather than kicked. Personally, I'm glad he did what he did; less pain for me.)

As I was getting up to deal with the second guy, the one I had been pummeling grabbed me by the waist and started to pull me down and him up. The second guy had disappeared all of a sudden, so I grabbed the guy who was holding onto me and slammed his head into the metal pole that was holding up the carport. This pretty much ended the fight with him. He went down and stayed there.

But sometime during this, my sweats were ripped. Not just a little tear—they ripped from the waist down the leg and dropped around my ankles. This was the time the second guy got back involved. He had run across the alley and brought a metal bucket back with him, swinging it like crazy. As I was getting out of the way of a wide swing of the bucket, the sweats tripped me up and down I went. The guy must've been a kickball champ as a kid, because he started playing kickball with me again. I did about the only thing I could do with my feet tangled—I rolled and got over to a parked car. He let up

190

for a minute and I was able to get around the car and stand up. I pulled up my sweats, but I had to hold them or they would be back around my ankles. He yelled, "You better run, or I'll kick your ass!" But he didn't start to come around the car. Frankly, I was a little stunned. I was mad because he had given me a couple good kicks and I hadn't gotten to hit him back. I was sure I could take him, but I didn't want to strip to my briefs to do it. While I stood there trying to decide if I should rip the sweats off and go after the SOB, he helped his friend up and into their car and sped off.

I went back to my apartment and noticed that my watch was missing. So I went back out and found it lying there with a broken band. Then I went in and took care of my cuts and scratches. Some I got from the ground, others from his kicks. I had a couple bruises and bumps, but nothing serious.

Let's analyze the events that went down. First, you could argue that I shouldn't have gone out there in the first place. This is true, but I made the decision to go out. You'll have to make your own decisions.

So since I did go out and I was expecting trouble, there are a few things I should have done. It would have taken only a second or two to change into jeans and to take my watch off. This would have eliminated the broken watch problem and the ripped sweats. With jeans instead of the ripped sweats, I wouldn't have been tripped up like I was. This would have put things much more in my favor, and I wouldn't have had to deal with the frustration of getting kicked in the head without being able to retaliate. I had the option of choosing what I would fight in, and I ignored the opportunity to change.

My buddy Jeff got into a fight one night in Fayetteville while wearing a toga. (It was the required dress at the party he was attending.) Of course, the toga didn't last long, and Jeff was out in the middle of the yard pounding on this guy wearing nothing but his Fruit of the Looms. So sure, I could have

191

ripped my sweats off and chased the guy while wearing my briefs. And if he had pursued me, I would have had no choice but to pound on him while in my underwear. But the truth is I was hesitant because of my absence of pants, and the guy helped his friend up and left. I can think of a lot of things I should have done now, but I should have been thinking more before I went outside.

There's also the fact that I was going outside to face two people by myself, but I'll address this in another chapter. This chapter is just to get you to think a little about what you are wearing and what the strengths and weaknesses of your choice of clothing are.

NOTES

1. Animal and I joke that besides both of us having lost watches in fights, we've both had watches eaten by the same dog: Tim's.

WALLS, STAIRS, AND SUCH

"In this job, I won't take a second-place

man. Second place is a body bag."

—Gy.Sgt. Carlos Hathcock

to the first marine sniper

class at Quantico

I remember one time when my dad was telling me about a guy he had a conversation with. Dad said that after the guy was thrown down a flight of stairs and then thrown back up them he started to listen. This brings us to a few of our most available weapons: walls, stairs, windows, and the floor or ground. Maybe you don't want to really consider them weapons, but they can certainly aid you in damaging someone.

I guess I learned the usefulness of stairs when I was in junior high. I was the new kid at school and got the usual "trying out" of students that age. On one such occasion—and the last—I threw Roger, the biggest kid in the class, down the stairs. He was bigger than I was, so I needed some way to even the score. Since we were on the second floor near the stairs, well? This actually earned the respect of Roger and the other "toughs," and I was one of the "in" crowd from then on. Actually, Roger and I became very good friends after that.

Years later, I was still throwing people down the stairs every now and then. While on CQ (Charge of Quarters) one time at Ft. Bragg, I told a guy who was drinking and causing a disturbance in the barracks to knock it off. Instead of listening, he got in my face and started to mouth off. I really wasn't in the mood for his acting up, so I grabbed him, pulled him to the stairwell, and pushed him down the stairs. I grabbed him where he had stopped halfway down and bounced him the rest of the way down. I then marched him to the front door and tossed his ass out of the barracks, and then down the entrance steps. It was this last part that the first sergeant of the neighboring company witnessed, and he came over to see what was going on.

I told him who I was and that I was on CQ, and then I relayed the circumstances that led to what he had witnessed. He said, "Very well," and turned to the guy I had thrown out. "Soldier, I recommend that you straighten your ass out before you try to go back into that building." Then he left.

Yes, stairs can come in handy. A tumble down a flight or two can take the fight out of a guy pretty easily. A word of caution, though—just falling on the ground or floor can hurt a person very seriously. Falling down a flight of stairs can end up very serious indeed. I could have found myself in a lot of trouble if the individual I tossed out had gotten seriously injured. People working in positions like bouncers, security, CQ, and so on need to use control in handling people to ensure that those they are handling do not get injured. Otherwise lawsuits arise. That's what all those "necessary force" laws and rules are about. If I were in the same situation today, I would handle it differently.

On the other hand, in a self-defense situation, by all means use what you have available. Knock him down the stairs and then take off. Remember, there are no rules in a street fight.

As handy as stairs, and usually a lot more available, are walls. Walls can be very useful, and I have used them in many different incidents. One such time was a way to teach a guy not to smoke in my room. I'm not a smoker, so I asked people not to smoke in my room in the barracks I lived in, as well as my apartments, houses, and so on. Most people had no trouble with this request. Well, one day a group of us were gathered in my room of the barracks at Bragg to watch a movie. As I was putting the video into the VCR, I heard someone behind me say, "You better not light that in here." A new guy in the company was about to light up.

"Why not," he asked, sort of defiantly.

"Because it's my room and I don't like anyone smoking in here," I answered. I then turned back to the VCR. All of a sudden the room got deathly silent and I caught a whiff of smoke. He had lit up anyway.

I'm sure he was the only one in the room who wasn't expecting the explosion that was my reaction. I turned, took a step toward him, and grabbed onto his shirt. Before he realized what was happening, I was pushing him full force out the door. We stopped when he slammed into the wall across the hall. It knocked the wind out of him and he just sort of stared at me with a blank look on his face. I told him he wasn't allowed back into my room and turned and shut the door on him.

You see, walls can be used for more than hanging pictures on and keeping the roof up. I never hit him, I just escorted him out of my room. It was the wall that knocked the wind out of him.

Walls are also very good to slam people against when you need to get their attention during an important discussion. I talk about this in the chapter on chokes and sleepers. You can also use them just to bounce a guy off of a few times to inflict pain and punishment.

I remember the time I met my friend Eric walking a guy up the street with his hands around the dude's throat. Every few feet he would stop and slam the guy against the wall they were walking beside.

"What's up?" I asked.

"Caught this son of a bitch trying to break into my hooch," he replied. (We called the little places we lived off post in Korea hooches.) He was taking the guy to the S-5 office. They were the authorities that handled such complaints involving Koreans and U.S. soldiers, as well as a whole slew of other problems. I happened to be friends with the sergeant on duty at the S-5 office—we had been in the same company at Bragg—so I tagged along.

When the S-5 sergeant asked Eric how come the guy looked beat up, Eric replied, "He fell."

Jim looked at me and asked, "Burrese, I suppose you saw it?"

"Yeah, he fell," I answered.

Eric and I left the guy at the S-5 office and went off down the street. He filled me in on what had happened and that one of them had gotten away. He then went home, and I finally got back to my buddies, who were waiting on me for more drinks. (I had been on a beer run when I met Eric bouncing the guy off the wall.)

Besides showing how a wall can be used, this story also illustrates the benefit of having a friend as a witness and knowing the right people.

You can make things uglier by using a wall with some sort of window. Broken glass can get real nasty. My dad once showed a bully the folly of his ways by slamming him into a wall. It just so happened that the wall he chose happened to be in front of a movie theater, and the spot he chose was where one of the movie poster windows was. It definitely got the point across, and the bully had a sudden change of heart. It's funny how that usually happens when someone finally stands up to those kinds of people.

Another word of caution: you can mess yourself up when throwing someone through a window. A fellow sniper cut his arm pretty severely one night in Seoul when he threw an opponent through a glass door during a big brawl. Sure, the other guy was much worse off, but my friend's arm was out of commission for quite a while.

Just because I use the word "wall," don't get too narrow of a definition of the term. Any object that is standing vertical to the ground can be used. Slamming someone into a car, telephone pole, wall-locker, etc. can have the same results. Use what is available. If I have a choice between punching an opponent with my fist or slamming him into some immovable object, I'll take slamming him into something every time. You can do more damage, in less time, with less pain to yourself.

Mike Haynack showed this in the video *Barroom Brawling* very well. He slammed his opponent into a wall and then smashed his face into a pool table. Why spend time punching and kicking when you can end it real quick with a wall or other immovable object. Slamming a person's body into a wall is much safer than driving a dude's head into something. The header should only be used for dire emergencies.

It also only makes sense to use walls when you are in tight quarters. You might not have the room to dance around and use your fancy spinning back kicks. So slam the dude's face into a wall and get out of the area.

The last thing I want to talk about in this chapter is something you will always have available, the ground or floor. I wrote a little on this in the chapter "to the ground," but I'll mention a bit here.

The ground is about as immovable as you are going to get. If you start slamming a person's head into the ground, I guarantee his head will fare far worse than the sidewalk or street. This can be very effective and very deadly.

This isn't a very fancy or pretty technique that will win points in a contest, but it can end combat real quick-like. If you are on top and can grab your opponent's head, a smash into the pavement will usually end the encounter. If he has long hair, it makes his head easier to grab onto. Grab as much as you can down close to the roots, and give everything you've got into making his head connect with the concrete. This can be very ugly and cause severe injury, so it should only be done in severe circumstances.

Just as you can end a fight this way, so can your opponent. Do everything you can to keep him from getting a hold of your head. Protect your head and neck at all costs.

Walls, stairs, and the ground can be your allies in a fight if you use them, and they can be your enemies if your opponent uses them against you. So remember, use them before he does!

FIGHTING MORE THAN ONE

CHAPTER 20

"We cannot do everything at once, but

we can do something at once."

—Calvin Coolidge

Remember the movie *Billy Jack*? Billy was bad, but he still got stomped good when he went up against a group of guys. More often than not, this is the case when a person is outnumbered. The odds are with the group. The single best reaction when facing multiple opponents is to get out of Dodge or recruit some help. If neither of these options is available to you, you may be in a whole heap of trouble, especially if you go to the ground. While you're lying there trying to cover your vital parts, the group is going to be wearing out boot leather as they kick and stomp on your poor old body. This is definitely a situation to avoid at all costs. Fighting one person is danger-ous enough, but facing more than one intensifies the situation and increases the likelihood of your getting seriously injured.

There are some steps you can take to increase your chances of not being seriously injured when going up against multiple foes. I'll talk a little about some of the things you should consider when faced with this situation.

TRAINING

Yep, we are back to this again. Are you getting the point that if you get into a fight, it's the training you have done beforehand that will be one of the things that aides you the most? (Right after experience and the proper mind-set, accom-panied by sheer determination to win, of course.)

While I was stationed at Ft. Bragg, I used to train some down at Wolf's Karate Studio on Yatkin Road. Mr. Wolf believed in mixing it up—no paper tigers there. We would do a lot of contact sparring, and it wasn't uncommon for people to end up with black eyes, fat lips, and bloody noses. It was all in the fun of training, and we did try to be careful not to hurt anyone seriously. (You don't want to lose all of your training partners.) But there were a lot of people who never came back after their first class of mixing it up. I took a couple of real good groin shots during that training, and it sure did get me thinking about my defenses. Funny how you remember the pain more than someone's words. It hurts just thinking about it, and that was a long time ago.

Mr. Wolf also liked to pair us up against each other in odd-numbered groups—two against one, three against two, and three against one at times. I liked this training and found it to be useful for both groups. When you are on the side with the number advantage, it is easy to get into each others' way at times. Sometimes it's hard to attack with three at once. So you learned how to work in a group, and you discovered what you wanted to do to members of a group you're against by being on the other side. But it was definitely the person by himself who got most of the workout. You had to be on your toes at all times, and when one of your opponents was taking a couple of quick breaths, his buddy or buddies would be attacking you. So the guy alone had no breaks. When it was two against another number, you learned to watch each other's back and work as a team. Yes, that was some fun and valuable training.

We used to always team up against each other in our barracks' wrestling matches, and we had some awesome king-of-the-hill competitions, too. Who says soldiers don't know how to have fun? All of these things hone the skills you need when you're faced with multiple attackers. So if you haven't done this kind of training, start. As I've said throughout this book, nothing beats experience and training. You can't just read about it or watch it on a video. You must get out there and train, and train hard.

Serious

When you are outnumbered and it's just a fight, not combat, the odds are that you're going to get a good beating, but not much more. Unless, of course, it gets broken up. I had one of these that was actually pretty fun when I look back on it, but was I angry at the time.

A bunch of guys were throwing people into the small creek behind our barracks in Korea. Usually I would join in on such activities, but on this particular evening I was showered and ready to go downrange. I didn't want to get my clothes dirty and then have to get all cleaned up again; people were waiting on me. Well, a couple guys from a different platoon decided differently. I told them I wasn't involved and if they tried to get me involved I was going to throw down. So this E-

6 who didn't care for me a whole lot started to mouth off about how I wasn't as bad as people said I was, and I definitely wasn't as tough as *I* thought I was. Hey, everyone is entitled to their opinion. Often, this kind of comment set me off immediately, and I'd throw down to prove the loud-mouth wrong. However, on this night I didn't want trouble, I just wanted to give my roommate a message and then head down town to Tokori and hook up with Brian and Frank.

But this dude wasn't going to let me. He confronted me, and as I was trying to talk my way out of it, two of his buddies rushed me from behind and grabbed me. Boy, did I let loose. I was kicking, kneeing, elbowing, and punching anything I could reach. A couple more of his goons joined in, and it wasn't too long before some of my platoon members came over to break things up. All said and done, there were some bumps and bruises on both sides, but nothing serious. Except the brand new shirt I was wearing and didn't want dirty was not only covered with dirt and some blood, but it was all ripped up too. That's what burned me up—I would have been better off letting them throw me in the creek.

Later that night some guy came up to me outside a bar downrange and said, "You're that guy who was throwing down outside of Charlie Company, aren't you?"

"Yeah, that was me."

"Man, you were kickin' some ass. It reminded me of back in Chicago. I want to buy you a beer."

"Sure, why not?" Who was I to turn down a free drink?

When you go into any physical confrontation, you need to explode all over your opponent. Nuclear, remember? When you are up against multiple attackers, it is even more crucial. You go from being one nuclear warhead to being ten. The only difference between this fight and if you are in a more serious confrontation is the kinds of blows you deliver. Above, I was only trying to give black eyes, bloody noses, and fat lips—and throw in a few good bruises for icing on the cake. In combat mode against more than one, you need to hurt people and hurt them bad. You finish them off so they're out of the fight. You don't give anyone a chance to get back into the ruckus.

My dad taught me this lesson a long time ago. The fight that landed him in a courtroom was just such an instance. He and his buddy were outnumbered, and their opponents were armed. (One of them, anyway, had a small sap.) Dad said he told the guy that he'd break his back if he swung his small implement. The guy swung and the battle was on. Dad broke the guy's back over the back of his truck and waded into the others. He said he and his buddy had no thoughts except to stop people, and the way to stop them was to hurt them seriously—grab hold of a guy and either break something or maim him to a degree that he wouldn't come back.

There's no time to mess around in a situation like this when it's for real. You give it your all and keep it up until there's no one left to maul or you're physically unable to continue. It's not a game, and it gets very ugly. The differences between my fight outside the barracks and the combat situation my dad was in at the drive-in are similar in some aspects, but very different in others. You need to explode in both, but the kinds of blows and the techniques you use are much different.

When you're fighting more than one, there's nothing wrong with going berserk on a guy just long enough to punch a hole and run. If you can get away, do so. If some of them pursue you, it's likely that some will stay behind to aid their injured buddy that you freaked out on. Those chasing may not be as eager to be the first to catch you after seeing how easily you just busted someone's leg. Make a hole, and get out through it.

EVEN THINGS UP

At the beginning of this chapter I said that the best thing to do was to scram or get some help when you're up against multiple attackers and outnumbered. That's true—having guys on your side is the best way to even things up. Sometimes when you're dealing with gangs or pack mentality, a showing of equal force on the opposition's side will make the aggressors back down.

There was a time in Dong Du Chong (aka Tong Du Chong or TDC) when Greg and a buddy were outnumbered four to two. A couple of Greg's friends showed up and evened things out. Lo and behold, the guys stopped talking tough and stopped provoking Greg into something. They were real bad when they had the upper hand, but as soon as things evened out they didn't want anything to do with any physical confrontation. Typical bully behavior, and packs or gangs are just like bullies, only they can be worse because of the numbers.

The other way to even up the sides is with weapons. Just like the old saying that Colt made all men equal, a weapon can even the odds right quick. A gun definitely evens the score, and I know several people who have pulled firearms on groups that were attacking them. This should only be done in extreme circumstances, for I believe you should only pull a gun if you are ready and prepared to shoot someone in order to save your own life. But it does work. When someone is looking down a barrel of a loaded weapon, he starts to wonder if he really wants to continue.

Other weapons will help even the score without the seriousness of firearms. If you are carrying a sidearm, you are going to have to explain why to the police later. If you grab a stick of some kind lying in the street, it's a lot easier to justify.

In the chapter on what you are wearing, I discussed an altercation I had with two guys outside of my apartment. I did some things wrong there. I shouldn't have taken the guy to the ground like I did and not be able to defend against the other guy. He came running up behind me and started kicking me in the head and back. Not good! The one thing I did do right was finish the first guy off quickly once I had the other one to contend with. Smashing his head into the iron carport post did the trick just fine. But by then it was too late, since my sweats were ripped and bunching around my ankles.

A few days after this had happened, I was visiting my dad. He asked what I had gotten into when he saw me a little messed up. I told him the story, and his reply was that since there were two of them I should have taken an ax handle or something with me. "Don't go alone and unarmed when you're outnumbered," he said.

I got a laugh out of him when I replied, "But there were only two of them." But I knew he was right. It probably wasn't the most intelligent thing I have ever done. My dad's friend, Jerry, said, "I don't even mess with that anymore. I have a .357 Mag to take care of any of that kind of business."

My dad answered, "Yeah, we're too old to mess around anymore."

It was some time later when I was telling Animal about the incident over the phone. When I was finished, he said, "Alain, when you are outnumbered, use a weapon."

"Yeah, that's just what my dad told me," I answered.

KEEP THEM AWAY

A good strategy to try and employ is to keep your attackers away from you. Don't let them all get a hold of your precious body. As I mentioned above, weapons are good at evening the score, and one of their uses is to keep the aggressors at bay. The trouble arises when someone gets inside your perimeter defense and ties the weapon up. (This is for extension weapons such as a club. Guns and knives aren't rushed as easily.) When one ties you up, the others can get in and do a number on you. So it's important to remain in control and use everything you have to keep them from closing.

You should also try and use your attackers against each other. Remember how I said that we would sometimes get in each other's way while attacking during our multiple-attack training sessions? That's what you want to cause among those you are facing. Move in such a way as to put them in line, so you are using one person to shield you from another. If you put a guy down, put him between you and his buddies. It will gain you a second or two as they try to get around him. Shoving someone into someone else also works to buy you a fraction of a second. That fraction may be all you need to get out of the area.

As a last note on fighting multiple attackers, I stress again that the best thing to do is escape. The odds are with the numbers, and there's no embarrassment in hitting the road to save your hide. If you do have to fight, give it all you have. Try not to go to the ground, and if you do, protect your vital areas, especially your head. Get back to your feet if you can, and do it quickly. Your mental attitude is crucial. Sheer determination and ruthlessness will be critical in this type of battle. It's your determination that will get you off the ground and see you through to the finish.

DRUNKS

CHAPTER 21

"You ain't big enough, and you

don't have enough friends."

—Me, joking and for real

on a number of occasions

Alcohol, that wonderful substance that has been around for ages and has been messing up people's minds and making them act stupid for just as long. Right up front, I don't drink much and I never have. I'm not here to tell you how much you should or shouldn't drink; I'm just going to tell you a few things that are alcohol related with regard to the area of fighting and keeping from getting squashed or stomped.

Since a high portion of fights occur in bars, saloons, taverns, and other joints that serve alcohol, it's not surprising that many of those engaged in the fighting are under some influence of the nectar of the

207

gods. So let's talk a little about fighting drunks, fighting while drunk, and other related matters.

FIGHTING DRUNKS

I was BSing with Greg one day about some of the fights that went down in Korea. I remember him saying, "Most of the time I was just stomping drunks. It makes it so much easier when they're drunk. I guess on the other side, that's a good lesson to not get in a fight when you're drunk. You'll be the one getting stomped."

I couldn't agree with this more. It is so much easier to beat some drunk than it is to fight someone sober. That is one of the reasons I didn't drink much when I went out to the bars. Actually, there were a few reasons: I didn't like wasting money on booze, I usually was the one driving home so that none of us would get in trouble or killed, and if anything went down, I liked to be in control so that I could handle the situation. Whether fight or flight, I was ready.

I don't care who the person is, he isn't going to be able to fight better while drunk. Sure, I've heard the loud-mouths: "I fight better when I'm drunk—bring 'em on." That's bullshit! It is proven that alcohol slows down your response time, thinking capabilities, and motor skills. These are all extremely important during a physical encounter. The more alcohol a person has had and the more drunk he is, the slower he's going to be. Sometimes it gets pretty ridiculous. If you've ever seen someone who is sober just manhandle a drunk like he was a child, you know what I mean.

I've had drunks throw punches at me that were so slow and telegraphed that I could have yelled over to a buddy, "Watch me duck this punch and squash this guy!" before I even started to move. I'm serious, I've seen guys get pulverized while hardly throwing up any resistance. Oh, they thought they were, and they had talked like they would, but they were just too drunk to do anything but run off at the mouth.

So yes, fighting against someone who is drunk is often a lot easier than fighting someone who is sober. I've had many times where I'd remark, "This will be easy, he's drunk." (Never take that for granted, though. Some dudes can be bad mothers even when drunk, and they are only worse when sober.)

You might think by my attitude that I'm against drinking and being drunk. On the contrary, I have nothing against drinking and the effects, as long as the person doesn't turn into a belligerent jerk. That's where I have the big problem and a low tolerance level. There isn't much that annoys me more than some drunk acting up and bothering others. Now, being loud and stupid and having a good time is one thing. That I don't mind. It's the drunks who get real obnoxious and start wrecking things or bullying people. I don't care for bullies one bit. And the son of a bitches who start treating women badly really get to me.

I'll describe a real typical scenario that took place quite often in Korea. I'd be in one of the local bars with a few friends playing pool. Usually it was Frank and Brian, and often there would be another guy or two with us. For a guy who doesn't drink much, I've spent a lot of hours in bars. I liked the company, and it was something to do. Usually we'd have a pool table and Brian would be beating all of us in eight ball, or nine ball, or any other game of billiards we wanted to try our hand in.

Everything would be fine, and then came the drunks who didn't know how to act like human beings. Like I said, I didn't mind people being loud and having a good time. It was when they started messing with people or especially the women working the bars. In my book, a woman is a woman; I don't care if she's a bar girl, waitress, or the president of some company. You treat them all well.

Since there were a few bars that we frequented more than the rest, we knew all the girls who worked in these places. We liked them and they liked us. So when some dickhead or dickheads started to give them a hard time, it got on my nerves. Now these were girls who had been around awhile, and they could handle themselves around GIs pretty well, but I still didn't like it. So if it started to get a little out of hand, I'd go over and have a talk with the above mentioned.

Usually, I'd be nice at first and just ask them to settle down a bit. I'd usually say the girl was a friend of mine and ask them to lay off. You know, a lot of the time this worked and nothing else was needed. I don't know if it was my charming personality or the fact that they could sense that I'd go off at the drop of a hat. Lack of fear, or at least not showing fear, has a way of putting bullies in their place. Guys who mess with women are just a form of bully in my book, only worse. I'm sure having Brian and Frank standing over by the pool table, annoyed that our game had been interrupted, didn't hurt either. Frank has told me that I have a look that means business and can scare people, but Brian's is worse. When you look at him when he's ready for business or mad, you know you don't really want any of that.

These are the kinds of drunks I don't care for. So if you drink, have fun and live it up—just respect other people and don't be an ass. The world has far too many as it is; we don't need any more. In his column in *Musclemag International*, Dave Fisher stated that he'd like to see a lot of the bodybuilders out there stop being jerks. One comment was, "Stop going to bars to beat up guys who weigh 60 pounds less than you do because it really doesn't make you look so tough—contrary to what you thought." I'm with Fisher. Grow up!

FIGHTING WHILE DRUNK

I've said that when you are drunk you can't fight as well,

and that's true. Some people, however, can handle themselves well while inebriated, and you can increase your level of effectiveness while intoxicated with some work. (Oh, great, now I'm telling drunks how to fight better.)

My buddy Jeff at Bragg could handle himself both sober and intoxicated. Frankly, Jeff would stomp people even while he was drunk off his ass. Remember, I said there were guys like that. Take that night at a Fayetteville house party when Jeff was out in the middle of the front yard wearing only his white Fruit of the Looms, beating some guy into the ground for messing with some girl. It wasn't because of being drunk that Jeff wasn't dressed; his toga had been ripped off. But he was drunk and still pounding this guy. So some people can fight when intoxicated, and some do it very well. I'll tell you, though, Jeff was even more formidable when sober.

So how do you fight better when drunk? A lot of it has to do with your ability to handle alcohol. You probably know that alcohol affects different people differently. It has to do with your size, your drinking experience, and your chemical makeup. Some people can consume a whole lot more than others. Some folks get mean; others get silly. Some just get plain stupid. So in a sense, you can't do much about part of it. Some guys can just fight better drunk than others.

You can improve what you have to work with, though, simply by practicing drunk. Animal and I were BSing about this one day, and he said, "Yeah, if you fight a lot when you're drunk, you should practice drunk." It's the same as practicing in alleys, on stairs, in crowded rooms, and anywhere else that makes your training more realistic. If you fight drunk, practice drunk once in a while.

You can make it a hell of a lot simpler by just not fighting. But hey, these are your choices. I'm just giving you a few tips.

One thing I will say. Yes, you can improve your fighting-while-drunk skills by doing it. This is the case with many skills. But don't go out and think you can improve your driving-while-drunk skills. This is a real sore spot for me. I've had a couple of friends killed by drunk drivers, and I frown on that activity greatly. One was a girl who was a close friend and had a lot going for her. A drunk ran a red light and hit her and the guy she was with. They were on a motorcycle and the drunk driver was in a pickup. Not too difficult to see who got the worst of that one. I guess that's one of the reasons I've stayed sober and been the designated driver so often.

Anyway, drinking is fine. Just don't drive, don't be a jerk, and preferably, don't fight.

WEAPONS

"Don't pack hardware for

bluff or balance."

—Ken Alstad

Savvy Sayin's

This by no means is an exhaustive diatribe on the use of weapons. I'm no expert in their use, and if I were, I couldn't do justice to weapons instruction in one chapter. I'm going to briefly say a few words concerning the use of weapons in fighting. These are just a few of the things I've experienced and believe to be true.

WEAPONS IN GENERAL

When I say weapons, I mean anything that can aid you in defending yourself from your attacker. This includes just about everything: rocks, keys, pool cues, bottles, trash can lids, buckets, and of course, knives and guns. Buckets, you say? Yes, I've had one swung at my head. Not one of those plastic types, but a good solid steel one.

The thing about weapons is that they escalate the conflict into another realm of seriousness. Yes, a person can inflict a lot of damage with his bare hands, including killing a person. But with weapons, this becomes far easier. Especially with guns—anyone can pull a trigger. I say anyone as in physically being able to squeeze off a round. The psychological aspects of shooting someone are a whole different story.

One concern you will face in the event you use a weapon in a confrontation is that of the law. Why were you carrying the weapon in the first place? This is something that may come back to haunt you. Many weapons that you may carry have no other purpose than to injure or kill someone. You'll have to explain why you were carrying it after you use it. If you weren't out to kill someone, why were you packing a weapon? "Just in case," or "to protect myself" aren't the best responses at times. Most of the time I don't bother carrying a weapon because of the potential legal trouble it can land you in.

I also think that many people who carry weapons for self-defense get complacent and do things that they would otherwise avoid because of a false sense of security offered by a weapon. I remember a group of women I was talking to once. I was stressing the importance of awareness and avoidance when one woman stated, "I don't worry about that because I carry this." She held up a small canister of mace or some other related chemical spray. I quickly pointed out to the group that this was just the kind of attitude I was stressing should be avoided. I told them about a friend of mine, Mike, who used to spray the stuff into his own face and say, "This isn't so bad." Sure his eyes were watering, but he was far from incapacitated. He was definitely functional. A weapon does not replace the need for being aware of what's going on and avoiding trouble in the first place.

This brings me to another important fact that many people forget when dealing with weapons. A weapon does not replace thinking and all the other tools at your disposal. Just because a guy has a knife in his hand, it doesn't mean that he won't hit you with the other. On the contrary, if he knows what he's doing he'll be sure to use everything he has available. If you are using a weapon, don't forget the rest of your options—and the limitations of your weapon.

All weapons have their limitations. It is a good idea to study the various kinds of implements and their strengths and weaknesses. There are proper defenses against almost all weapons, and you should be familiar with and practice these if you plan to go up against an armed assailant. I say almost all, because unless you are expertly trained, I advise against going up against someone with a firearm. Yes, there are weaknesses in using a gun, and you can take a firearm away from a person with the proper training. But this is very risky business, and usually the risk isn't worth the reward. If the reward is just keeping your wallet, you are a fool to risk your life over it. On the other hand, if you are certain that the assailant intends to kill you no matter what, you may opt to try a practiced disarmament technique if the opportunity arises.

Since I just mentioned disarmament techniques, let's examine them a bit. There are countless books and articles out there that demonstrate how to take a weapon away from an attacker. I'm going to give you the best defense you have when unarmed against an armed assailant. As soon as you recognize that you are about to be assaulted with a weapon and that you are unarmed, turn and run in any direction that will get you out of the area unscathed.

This is the single best defense against a weapon, even a gun. The more distance you put between you and the armed person, the less chance you have of being injured. Every step you put between you and a gunman lessens the possibility that he can hit you if he opts to shoot. It is extremely hard to hit a moving target anyway, and most muggers are not marksmen or trained shooters.

Okay, what if for some reason you can't run away? Maybe you have to stay to protect someone, or maybe you just decide to fight for whatever reason. It's your choice. Many of the disarming techniques that are shown in self-defense books just don't work against an experienced knifer or gunman. As for clubs and other weapons, I'm not quite as hesitant to go up against someone with one of these. But knives and guns get messy, and you are in for a real surprise when the attacker doesn't do any of the things you need him to do to perform your "never fail" technique. There is no such thing, and someone who knows what he's doing won't allow you to do all the fancy fantasy stuff taught in a lot of so-called self-defense books. On the other hand, many people who wield weapons are not trained and actually are pretty sloppy. Their only training comes from watching martial art videos. These people can be disarmed if you know what you are doing. The key is to learn from a competent instructor and learn techniques that have been proven in real situations. Don't forget to train for things that will go wrong, because they will.

That's a little general information. Now let's look at a few specific weapons and things about them.

CLUBS AND SUCH

One of the common instruments you may wind up facing is the old-fashioned club. This could be in the form of a pool cue, baseball bat, or any other such object. The key to defending against one of these is to get inside of its effective range. There is a spot a few inches from the top of the striking weapon that is the most dangerous to be hit by. In baseball they often call this the sweet spot, and it's where you want to connect with the ball. The heavier the instrument, the slower it will be to reverse directions. If a guy swings a bat at you, you want to be just outside of its range as it passes. Then you have time to be all over the guy before he can reverse the weapon and gain momentum in the other direction. That's why someone trained in the use of a staff or jo won't be swinging wildly. Fortunately, most people swinging things in bars aren't trained.

KNIVES

Right up front, knives are real ugly. Especially if the wielder of the knife knows what he's doing. The lucky thing is that a lot of people who pull a knife in a fight aren't knife fighters. The guy I mentioned in Chapter 15 ("Fast and Furious") who pulled a knife on my dad and his friend was not a knife fighter. If you are trained, you will be able to recognize someone who knows what he's doing versus someone who has watched a lot of TV.

I don't have a lot of experience with knives and am currently learning and training in their use. The two instances I have been in that involved a knife were pretty simple. In one, a guy said he had a knife and when he reached for something I clobbered him. I don't know if he actually had a blade or not. He said he did, so I hit him before he had a chance to prove it, and then I split. The other time, I used a chair on the guy. He pulled the blade and obviously didn't really know what he was doing. He was holding it out in front of him and slashing around with it. I grabbed a chair and pushed it at him legs first. I then threw the chair at him and exited the bar real quick. No sense hanging around for the MPs.

Neither of these guys was an experienced knife fighter. Someone who knows what he's doing won't let you know he has a blade until it's too late. He also won't lead with the knife. He'll protect it and use his free hand to hit you or set you up. However, even an amateur can get lucky. It doesn't matter if the guy is intentionally trying to slice you or just flailing around trying to keep his balance because you just pulled some fancy kung fu move. A cut is a cut. Get the weapon away from you, and keep it away.

If you want to become proficient in the art of knife fighting, you need to learn from a qualified instructor and practice. Naturally, I recommend Marc "Animal" MacYoung as an instructor. He has a book and a couple of videos out that have a lot of valuable information on knife fighting, but nothing replaces actual instruction. Check out attending one of his classes (you can write to him in care of Paladin Press).

There are also a lot of opinions on what kind of knife is the best for self-defense and fighting. It really depends on the person and the situation. The carrying of knives involves many different considerations. What is comfortable? What does the law say? What are you using it for? Where are you carrying it? What are you wearing?

I think the best advice is to pick a blade that is comfortable and fits the situation you are carrying it in. I really like my Cold Steel Tanto, and I carried it in the field when I was in the army. But it's a little big to carry in many circumstances. Often I carry my smaller Cold Steel Voyager. It's a folding tanto. As you may have noticed, I like the Asian style of blade. That's just my personal preference. I have a number of other knives, and they all have their own special uses and functions. A knife is just a tool, and you'll use it for many things other than combat. So pick something that feels right for you.

If you are serious about knives, you may want to invest in a good custom-made blade.[1]

GUNS

Guns are the great equalizers, and as I mentioned in the chapter on fighting multiple opponents, I know several people who have pulled guns to protect themselves. I don't believe in pulling any weapon for bluffing purposes. If it scares your attacker off, great. But don't count on it. If you are going to pull a gun on someone, you'd better be prepared to use it, and this means quite possibly killing someone. Unfortunately, shooting for center mass is often lethal; more than likely you will kill your opponent. If it comes to the point of you needing to defend yourself with a firearm, we are in the realm of deadly force. The people I mentioned above had every intention of blowing the person into the afterlife, because they were protecting their families.

You also need to know the laws of the state you are in. Each state has different self-defense and deadly force laws, and it would be beneficial to check them out. It could save you a lot of trouble later. You need to discern when it is appropriate to use deadly force. A person can't get carried away and shoot someone when they become excited and imagine a threat that really isn't.

I'm not advocating the possession of firearms for self-defense one way or the other. I do believe that if a person does decide to own a firearm, he should also be trained in its use. This is a must! One shooting accident is too many. I remember Eric's reaction upon learning that a shooting accident up at the DMZ in Korea was caused by an NCO. "He should lose his stripes," he exploded "There's no reason for such a thing—it's stupid carelessness."

It's true, the incident above was just carelessness. The NCO who was careless put a bullet through his own hand and into the wall right next to my roommate, who almost soiled his pants.

219

The buying of a firearm should be accompanied by a course in the proper safety and handling of such a weapon. If the weapon is going to be used in self-defense, by a civilian or someone whose job may require it, additional training is required. Formal instruction at a shooting school that includes combat applications is your best choice for learning defensive weapons skills. Just being a marksman is not enough. There are psychological aspects of shooting that need to be addressed. The top schools include this kind of training. Many people who are expert marksmen miss their game on hunting trips. This is referred to as "buck fever" and is common among inexperienced hunters. Shooting a human being is much more psychologically stressful, and without the proper training and mind-set, you are apt to miss your target completely.

There are a number of good shooting academies in the country, most of which screen their applicants. They specialize in training people who carry guns for a living, and it would behoove anyone to receive instruction before carrying a firearm for any reason.

IMPROVISED WEAPONS

The last thing I want to mention about weapons is that you need to be aware of what's in your environment that can aid you in a physical encounter. If you don't have a conventional weapon to use in defending yourself, you may have access to many environmental weapons. In fact, you usually have potential weapons all around you. I have to hand it to the guy who was swinging the bucket at my head in the alley—he was thinking and improvising.

Just pay attention to what's around you and to how it may be used in a self-defense situation. Remember, it's your mind that's your primary weapon, and if you use it, you'll find that you usually have more options available than you think.

NOTES

1. I personally like the knives of James S. Piorek. His company, JSP Blade Rigger, is located in Missoula, Montana, and he makes some exceptional blades as well as some very innovative harnesses and carrying rigs. Many of his knives are Asian in design, which I prefer. But he can do custom work to your specifications. He will also tailor a harness to fit your preferred blade and handgun, whichever you want. You can contact James at P.O. Box 5032, Missoula, MT 59806

WHEN, WHY, AND A WAY OUT

"It was involuntary.

They sank my boat."

—John F. Kennedy,

when asked how he had

become a war hero

If you haven't caught on by now, you probably won't. But I believe in avoiding confrontations, even though I didn't always do this. This part of the book addresses a couple of things. One, we do a lot of stupid things when we are younger, and hopefully we live through them to make it to old age. I also talk a little about when I feel it is justifiable to fight. I do believe it is necessary at times, just not as often as most people do. Some of this is because people get used to the thrill of fighting and even the thrill of combat, and they want to engage in these activities to experience their "high." I talk a bit about this and then discuss the benefits of realizing when you don't have to. There are so many better ways to relieve stress and spend your time. It's not up to me to tell you when to fight or when not to. Each person needs to make this choice himself.

If you are going through a period like I went through, I hope some of this will help you come out of it before something more serious happens. Learn as I did to channel things into a different, more positive direction. I hope some of this gets you thinking and will aid you in your own growth and development.

YOUNG AND STUPID

CHAPTER 23

"Know when to walk away,

know when to run."

—Kenny Rogers

The Gambler

I don't really know if it's stupid or that you just haven't learned enough yet. Stupid is when you don't learn from your mistakes, so maybe it's "young and not too smart yet."

Anyway, when I was younger, I definitely did some things that fall into the stupid category. Even as I was doing some of them I knew that I could be getting myself into a lot of trouble. Part of it's just growing up, and I suppose just about everyone has to find out some things for himself. Even after reading this, some will go out and do some of the things I describe as stupid. That's okay for those who get away with the stupid stuff like I did. Then they'll have some war stories to tell and something to laugh about later. For others, however, the lessons will be more serious. Prison, the hospital, and the morgue are possible ending places for certain stupid acts.

Sometimes it's fun to go looking for trouble. At times it's not really trouble you're looking for; you're just out looking for some good times and for something to alleviate the boredom of everyday life. Then again, you may be looking to blow off steam over different problems you're facing. To be honest, at times it's tough to figure out just why you do some of the things you do.

One night, my buddy Rhett and I were down in the bars on Hay Street in Fayetteville, North Carolina. We were two bad paratroopers out shooting the breeze and playing pool. Now, Hay Street had some of the sleaziest bars in Fayetteville, so naturally that's where we went to hang out. Most had some kind of dancers. Some were topless joints and others had girls who stripped to bikinis. Most had pool tables, toilets that would make you gag, and—in the better places—buckets to catch the water from leaking roofs when it was raining. A number of the bars employed Korean women. It was at such a place one night that Rhett and I decided to get extra stupid. Luckily, it didn't get as bad as it could have, or I wouldn't be writing this today.

We were playing pool and flirting with the dancers in one of the little dives we frequented. We decided to stop playing pool and enjoy the show while we had another beer. A Korean woman was dancing in a bikini, and after her set, she came over and sat with Rhett and me.

Rhett and I noticed two guys sitting across the bar. One was eyeing us pretty hard, the other was just sitting with him. When the girl left to wait on other customers, the bigger one, who had been glaring, walked over. "Watch what you two do with the girls," or something like that is what he said to us.

Now, this guy was big. But hey, we were sitting down; of course he'd seem big. And we were two all-American para-troopers—who did he think he was? We gave him a smart-ass, "Sure buddy, whatever."

He walked on by toward the john, and when he returned to his table, Rhett and I discussed how we'd handle the big SOB. A while later the guy's friend came over and apologized for the giant and said that it was just that he liked the one girl and was pretty protective. We shot back with, "Well, unless he wants a chair busted over his head he better watch himself."

Closing time! We were waiting around for the one dancer and were hoping to get a chance to talk to her and see what she was doing, when we noticed the big guy and his friend waiting around also. We were asked to leave again, so, undaunted, we strolled toward the exit where the other two were standing. I'm fairly short, only 5'9", but Rhett stands 6'2" or so, and this guy towered above him. I mean he was BIG. He was built like a professional wrestler—big all over. He had a gut on him, but you could tell he was also pretty powerful. He dwarfed Rhett and me.

No one said a word as we passed the two and went out into the street. They didn't follow us. We walked across the street to the parking lot where my truck was parked. We got in and watched the door of the bar we had just left. "What a fat-ass."

"Yeah, lucky for him he didn't get a bottle upside that big head."

"What do you want to do?"

"I don't know, what do you want to do? Bars are all closed. We could go get something to eat."

"I don't feel like going back to the barracks yet."

"Me either. Hey, she's leaving with him." The cute Korean was walking across the street toward the parking lot with the giant from the bar. The other guy had headed down the street the other way. They got into a car and started to pull away. "Let's follow them."

"Yeah."

So off we went. We weren't doing any of the tailing stuff that I had studied and practiced once in a while. We were blatantly obvious and right behind him.

Time out. Are the STUPID bells beginning to ring yet? They should be.

He made a few turns and we stayed with him, and shortly we were in a very bad neighborhood of Fayetteville and on a one-way street. He made a quick turn into a driveway and we went on by, only to realize we had to turn around and go back toward him. We turned around and started back as he screeched backwards and blocked our path.

It was at this moment that a whole bunch of ideas started flooding Rhett's and my thoughts. Things like, does he have a gun? He is pretty big. He knows there's two of us and he still wants to take us on. Someone protecting someone is more fierce than a couple of jerks out for kicks. We're in the wrong. This is STUPID!

I shifted into reverse and started to back up, he did the same, trying to corner us. "Shit," I said as I quickly determined which evasive maneuvers would get us out of there. As I turned to get past his car, the giant jumped out and lumbered toward my little truck. Rhett considered hitting him with the door as I sped past, but decided that I might get angry if it ripped the door off. Good choice—it probably would have come off, and yes, I probably would have gotten upset.

So we rode back to Bragg discussing how lucky we were. We didn't start talking about "what we would have done," etc. We knew we were pretty stupid and lucky that it hadn't been worse.

Two weeks later I found out just how lucky we had been. Jeff and I were in a different bar down on Hay Street. I was sitting at a video game, wasting my last quarter, as Jeff sat at a table beside me sipping a bottle of beer. I sensed someone standing beside me and noticed Jeff shifting positions. In less time than it takes to read this, I recognized that it was the giant from two weeks before who had walked up on me, and that Jeff, who realized it was the guy Rhett and I had talked about, was prepared to use the bottle for something other than to drink from.

"So, if it isn't the guy with the little red Ford. How is your truck these days?" As he said this my mind was racing: What am I going to do? What is he going to do? Did he mess with my truck? Probably not—he called it a Ford; I drive a Nissan. If he did, I'm coming back with the ax handle that's behind the seat. If he starts something, where's the nearest pool cue? These and many other thoughts quickly passed through my mind as I slowly stood. Jeff was paying close attention, and I knew he'd be there if needed.

As I looked up at the guy, he seemed even bigger than I remembered. Maybe it was because I was in a much mellower mood and hadn't had anything to drink. "It's just fine." I said, hoping that it still was.

"You're lucky I didn't have my gun that night. I would have filled that little truck with holes."

"Yeah, you're right. We were pretty stupid." I replied.

"You don't have to worry in here, I'm not going to start anything. It's out there," he pointed outside, "that you have to worry."

"You're right, we were wrong."

He nodded and walked toward the back of the bar. Jeff finished his beer and we went outside. "You weren't kidding, that was one big mother," he commented.

"Yeah, I just hope he didn't mess with my truck. If he did, we're going back."

We got to my truck and it was fine. I left Bragg for South

Korea shortly after that, so I never ran into the guy again. Rhett and Jeff never saw him either.

This story illustrates a couple different things. Let's look at them.

First, the giant walked the walk. He wasn't kidding when he said he would have used the gun if he'd had it with him that night. If you've been around a bit, you know when someone is running off at the mouth and full of hot air, and you know when he's not. That guy meant it. I meant it when I said we were lucky. We were!

Looking for kicks could have gotten Rhett and me shot or, at the least, a hole in my truck and the crap scared out of us.

As it was, I was also lucky that he didn't hold a grudge. It was stupid of me to be sitting in a bar and not paying attention to what was going on around me. My sitting there concentrating on an idiotic video game let him walk right up to me. Not that you should never play a video game or poker machine in a bar, but it hadn't been that long since our encounter. And when you do stupid things, you must be extra careful and increase your awareness. Having someone get the drop on you like that will do more for increasing your awareness levels than reading any book. As I said in the beginning, lessons learned the hard way are the ones that make the biggest impact. But sometimes they are the ones that hurt the most, too. Again, I was lucky that this lesson didn't hurt, and since that night, I pay more attention to who comes in and goes out of a joint.

He could have easily found my truck and vandalized it that night. This wouldn't have caused me any physical pain, but it would have hurt my wallet.

I'll mention another point here. If you do run around doing stupid things and getting into trouble, let those who run with you know also. That way things don't catch them unaware. Jeff knew about the run-in Rhett and I'd had with the guy, and he realized who it was as soon as the guy walked up to me at the video game. If something would have gone down, Jeff was ready.

This applies to other things as well. More than one person has found himself in trouble for something a friend has done that he knew nothing about. It's one thing if you're with someone and you know he has a trunk full of something illegal; it's another when you don't. ("Honest, officer, I didn't know he had the stuff." "Yeah, right. You want to make a statement?")

So, let those you run with know the score, and run with those who give you the same courtesy.

This incident didn't end up in a physical encounter, luckily, but many fights are over equally stupid activities. Most fights aren't really necessary when you analyze them. Big egos and a lot of testosterone are backing most fists that start flying.

I'll admit that I have always had a big ego. I like being in charge, I like winning, and I like things to go my way. All of this, combined with a very short fuse and a hot temper, have gotten me into trouble more than once. I was the type that, when someone said he would kick my ass, responded with, "Do it!" Often that was enough to get things started.

Most of the time it was stupidity on my part. I had something to prove. I don't know to whom, but I did. Other times I was just out looking for kicks or blowing off steam. Both of these can get you into serious trouble.

It's not much fun being spread-eagled against the back of a pickup with a cop pointing a loaded revolver at you, waiting for backup. We were just out for kicks, and when the cop pulled us over because he thought we looked suspicious (he was looking for alcohol), he found a gun my buddy kept under the seat. When it was all over, neither of us was in serious trouble, but my friend did have one of his handguns confiscated. The point is that the incident could have been avoided altogether if we'd used a little common sense.

231

I could go on and on about the stupid activities my friends and I have participated in throughout the years, and I'm sure you can probably think of many instances where you didn't really do the smart thing. But that's all in the past. The important thing is to recognize the stupidity and learn from it. It's repeating the same old things that is really stupid.

So start thinking about what you do for kicks and how you react in certain circumstances. A large part of it is just growing up and maturing. But it doesn't hurt to wise up early in certain areas.

Just remember, it only takes being unlucky one time and you won't have to worry anymore. I've learned to walk away from stuff and not blow up at insignificant events anymore. You can have fun without jeopardizing yourself or others, and differences can be resolved by means other than breaking bones. There are times when it's necessary to fight; just remember the words of my squash partner, John: "It hurts to be stupid."

SOMETIMES YOU HAVE TO

CHAPTER 24

"You can beat a man into submission,

but you can't change his mind."

—Something my father

always told me

There are some people out there—many, in fact, who believe that all fighting is inappropriate and that one should never fight. I disagree. Even though I stress the importance of not fighting and avoiding situations that lead to violence, I do believe at times it is necessary to engage in physical confrontations. I wish it weren't so, but it is. The important point is that it is up to you as an individual to decide when you should and when you shouldn't. Or when you have to and when you don't. I can't make that decision for you, and you and I may do things differently in the same situation.

All I can do here is give you a little advice and some things to think about.

Sometimes deciding whether to fight or not is a tough decision, and often you needed to make it yesterday. When things go down, you don't have much time to think about it anymore. You need to do whatever you're going to do immediately. So it pays to think about these things in advance so you know how to react in hazardous situations. You can't imagine every possible scenario, so you need to base your decisions on broader generalities. Like, I won't risk my life over the few dollars in my wallet, so I'll hand it over before I'll try to fight a mugger. Or, if someone lays his hands on me in a threatening way, I'll do whatever I can to stop him. Again, I won't tell you what choices to make. I'll just give you some of my thoughts and some things to think about. You have to live or die with your own decisions and choices. You see that word "die"? That's what makes these decisions so damn important.

A friend of mine was put into a tough situation a while back in Omaha. He was out of the army like me and getting his education with help from Uncle Sam. One night he and his younger brother were leaving a bar to head upstairs, where his brother was living at the time. They walked around a corner and came face-to-face with a guy holding a small automatic weapon similar to a MAC 10. At first, my buddy was thinking of doing something. Being a former infantry paratrooper with a Ranger tab, he wasn't one to scare easily, and he didn't really care for a guy pointing a gun at him and his brother. (When they walked around the corner, the guy immediately put the gun on them and said to do what he told them.)

However, he was unsure of what his brother would do, and anytime you go against someone armed with a gun, the odds are way in the gun wielder's favor. (Even if you can take a gun away from a guy, there is a high probability that the gun will go off in the process. The bullet may miss you, but who else is in the area?) He decided his best move would be to do what he was told, and it turned out that was the best course of action.

As he and his brother were turning toward the wall and kneeling as instructed, a second armed man came from the other direction. He was packing a semiauto handgun. If my buddy had tried to do something to the first mugger, the second guy would have had the drop on him.

The two demanded a car, and my friend turned over his keys. Then they marched my buddy and his brother into the bar and cleaned out the cash registers and all of the customers. The two crooks were calm and smooth; they had done this kind of thing before. The car was returned by the police the next day after it had been found abandoned across town. No one was hurt, and isn't that what you want in a situation like that?

Yeah, my friend said it was embarrassing to have it happen to him and that part of him wanted to take those two out. But he says the little embarrassment is a lot easier to deal with than if he would have done something and his younger brother had been killed. He also doesn't like the thought of his wife being a widow because he was trying to be a hero.

Let's look at another situation that happened in Butte, Montana. There was a guy who beat on his wife quite severely, but she would never do anything about it. People told her she should call the police and press charges, but she refused. One night, a bunch of people were hanging outside of a bar, saying good-byes and getting ready to head home, when the guy started smacking her around at the far end of the parking lot. One individual calmly walked over to his car, removed a crowbar, and walked over to the guy. Using the crowbar like a baseball bat, he struck the guy in the ribs. It dropped him immediately in pain. The individual with the crowbar then told the guy on the ground that if he ever hit his wife again he would kill him. It did end the beatings. I don't know how long the woman stayed with the guy after that; I think she should have left the first time he hit her and had him thrown in jail. But the beatings did stop. You see, bullies like that sometimes only listen to force.

As I've said, only you can decide when and why you should fight. In making that decision, you should ask yourself some questions.

What's the reason? Look at the real reason behind the confrontation. Is it because you are bored and looking for some action? Is it about your ego being hurt? Is it a serious threat to you or your loved ones? Is it to help a friend? (I personally will help a friend even if he was stupid to get into the mess in the first place.) Decide beforehand what reasons you'll fight for and what things you'll walk away from (or run away from at times).

What could happen? Look at the possible outcomes of the confrontation. Many small quarrels only end up in a few bruises or bumps. Not really a big deal. I've jumped in and broken up fights, even when I wasn't asked or paid to do it, when I knew I'd be able to handle the situation without any real risk to me. (After watching a couple guys go at it for a minute or two, you can tell whether they know what they're doing.) But if two guys are going at it with blades and I have no interest in the outcome and am not being paid to stop things, I'm not going to take the risk of getting poked for nothing.

My friend may have been able to take that gun in Omaha, but his brother could have been shot in the process. My friend could have ended up with a bullet hole also. Think about the possible outcomes and weigh the risks accordingly. Fighting is a lot like investing: everyone needs to determine what risk level they are willing to accept, and at what level will they bail. These levels are different for everyone.

What will happen if you don't? Just as important as looking at the possible outcomes if you do fight, you need to be aware of the possibilities of your not reacting. If all that's going to happen is you lose some money or material things, who cares? Those things are replaceable. But there's no way in hell I'll not react if it means physical harm to people I care about or to those who can't protect themselves. God help anyone who tries to rape or hurt a woman if I'm around. I become so infuriated when I read or hear about people being raped and assaulted in front of people who don't get involved. (I just become really pissed when I hear of rapes and assaults when no one's around.) If I ever come across a rape situation, it will be extremely difficult for me not to do something that would land me in big trouble (i.e., prison). And if it was someone I cared about, it would be ten times more difficult.

You need to consider what they may do to you also. I have a difficult time understanding the mind-set of so many of the Jewish people who were killed in the Holocaust. They were being led to slaughter in one of the greatest atrocities of this century, and they didn't fight back. My thinking goes more along the lines of taking a few with me if there is no other alternative. Like Billy Jack said in *The Trial of Billy Jack*: "If I'm going to get a beating, I might as well get in the first lick."

So remember to look at both sides of the situation. What will happen if you fight? And what will happen if you don't? And then you look for alternatives.

What are the alternatives? Besides just looking at fighting or not fighting in the situation, you should consider the other alternatives you have. Sure, at times there aren't many. If a guy jumps out of an alley and grabs you, you can fight, escape and run, or do what he says. But was there an alternative to walking where you were jumped? Do you see what I'm getting at? It all goes back to the awareness principles, being aware of everything. Many times in the heat of a situation our brains don't work the way we want them to. That is why it's so important to think about these things beforehand. It's the training and preparing you do now that will save your hide when things get ugly.

Run different scenarios through your mind. Talk and act them out with your training partners. Make decisions as to when it's appropriate to fight and when it's appropriate to run. Brainstorm alternate ways to deal with situations. Contact people who have been there and learn from them.

Any decision you make about anything should be based on intelligent information that you have gathered. When to fight is no exception. Base this decision on intelligent thought and not irrational ego trips.

When it's your job. I said earlier that I believe that at times it is necessary to fight. I don't believe anyone has the right to dominate another human being, and I'm all for an individual fighting back. As I've said, I hate bullies and feel that, at times, the only way you can teach these people the impropriety of their wrongful ways is by smashing them into the dirt. So much for all my communication and negotiation training in college. (We never discussed the boot-to-the-head method of conflict resolution in my conflict management class. Hmm.)

Besides these times, there is another time when, in my opinion, it is not only correct to fight, but your duty to. That is when you are being paid to handle confrontations and violent situations and you have exhausted all other possible means of handling the situation. I'm talking about soldiers, police officers, bouncers, security personnel, bodyguards, and people in other related occupations.

In the event of war, a soldier's duty is to protect the country. Soldiers have done this and will continue to do this by killing the enemy before the enemy kills them. But other occupations also involve physical encounters and, unfortunately, the taking of human life at times. There are times when police officers must use physical force to apprehend some of the scum that are out there preying on innocent folks. Bouncers and security personnel are also being paid to put themselves into harm's way to protect innocent people or establishments.

Again, you should exhaust your other means of diffusing the situation before you get physical. As I mentioned earlier, a good bouncer will stop confrontations before he gets to the point of blows when he can. A bodyguard will keep his client away from possible threats rather than play the hero during the attack. (Think about this one. Would you rather steer your client away from possible harm or take a bullet protecting him because you didn't avoid the situation?)

For this reason, I feel that people in these professions should engage in a regular program of exercise and in various forms of martial training. What I mean by martial training is any training that can be used in the hostile environments of the chosen profession. (Evasive driving skills, hand-to-hand combat, knives, marksmanship, batons, and so on should be included.)

The legalities and responsibilities of your position are important considerations when you become involved in confrontations while working. The time Dave and I tackled the guy in front of the dorm while we were working as night watch and Resident Assistant was a lot different than if we would have been downtown at a bar. Downtown, you have the option of getting out of the area before the cops come. I'm not necessarily recommending this; I'm just saying it's an option. You'll remember that earlier I mentioned that I told the guy that I'd have smashed his head against the sidewalk if we'd been downtown. If you're slammin' then scrammin', you can sometimes get away with this—as long as no one knows who you are. If they do, the police will just catch up to you later. And with the litigious society America has become, if you hurt someone, you are apt to be sued. (This is another reason it is important to fight only when it is absolutely necessary and to use only the amount of force that is warranted.) The possibility of being sued is even greater when you are working. Smashing the guy's head in front of the dorm would have landed both Dave and I in big trouble. So we restrained him and turned him over to the proper authorities.

Animal and I were discussing takedowns in the gym, and he was explaining the importance of protecting the guy you are throwing. In an alley, you can smash a guy's head and get away with it. If you are bouncing and you hurt someone, you and the joint you're working in can be hit with a lawsuit.[1]

A guy I used to work for in concert security has two lawsuits filed against him right now because of small injuries people incurred when things got physical. Employers don't like lawsuits. So besides the legal hassles it can cause you, you may also lose your job. (Remember the big bouncer in the movie *Roadhouse*? Yeah, it's a movie, but there were a few good points to be learned there.)

When all is said and done and something actually goes down, you need to remember that you have to do one thing or the other. If you're on the left side of the road you'll be fine, and if you're on the right side you'll be okay. But if you're somewhere out in the middle you're going to wind up squashed. Never go into it halfway. Make the decision and stick to it. As my buddy Frank says, "When you have decided that you're going to fight, explode on the guy(s). Don't mess around." Frank isn't talking about a firecracker, either, he's not even talking dynamite. Frank means go nuclear on the dude. Blast him with everything you have. Sure, when you're working there are the considerations I mentioned, but you still don't mess around. Get the situation under control; never be caught in the middle.

So yes, there are times you should fight. Whether it's because of your occupation or it's the decision you made with intelligent forethought, it's important to consider the things I mentioned in this chapter before you are faced with the situation on the street.

NOTES

1. I got to see Animal use one of these takedowns firsthand when we encountered a drunk at a place we were working in California. It was nice, and the guy didn't get hurt. We had to laugh at this guy. First he attacked some customers, then he attacked us, and then he went off on the cops who arrived. He lost all three times!

WHEN YOU WANT TO

CHAPTER 25

"Don't fight a battle if you don't gain

anything by winning."

—Gen. George Patton

Patton's Principles

This chapter is going to be foreign to many people. However, if you are reading a book such as this, there's a good chance you will know what I'm talking about.

There have been many times when I have wanted to fight—with no one person in particular. I just wanted to get into a fight with anyone. Some of you out there will relate to this, but remember, many people never have these feelings and don't really understand those who do.

I was talking to a friend once about what my father told me after I got into that fight with two guys behind my apartment. Dad told me I should have grabbed an ax

243

handle or something. My friend's reply was that his father would have told him to not go outside or to run. Neither he nor his father has ever been in an actual fight. Quite different from me and my father. It's a different way of looking at things, and I won't say either is right or wrong. I just happen to fall into the category that involved violence, and that is why I'm writing this. It's intended for those like me, or for those who want to better understand others.

The feelings of wanting to fight or engage in combat are not new. My father told me that he got to a point where nothing felt better than smashing someone. He looks back on these days now and wishes they wouldn't have happened. But they did, and he accepts that and is glad he has left that behind. I, too, experienced this "rush" after engaging in a battle. And yes, it is addicting like a drug.

People who don't understand these feelings will tell someone to go box, or practice karate, or do some other physical sport to fulfill the desire to gain the "rush." They think this is a good way to get over the feelings in a nondestructive way. Their intentions may be good, but the advice isn't. Sports are just not the same!

It's the "realness" of combat that gives the "rush." The knowing that you have to win in order to walk away. That's when the adrenaline starts pumping and the feeling of superalertness comes into being. I said it wasn't a new feeling, and it's not.

There have been references to these feelings in popular movies and books. Remember Clint Eastwood in *Any Which Way You Can*? There's the line in the bar where Clint's future opponent says, "You're addicted to the pain; you eat it like candy." I was watching the movie with my dad, and he quietly said, "Yeah, that's right." Later, I found out what my dad meant when I started to have the same feelings. In the previous movie, *Every Which Way but Loose*, Clint stated that at one time he liked fighting more than anything—well, almost anything. Yep, I know the feeling.

Another character that showed some of these feelings is *Rambo*. Now, before you balk, let me say that you should read the book from which the screenplay was adapted. The original book, *First Blood*, was written by David Morrell back in 1972, way before Sylvester Stallone made the character popular in the movies. I like Stallone's action movies, but let's face it, there's not a lot of reality there. The book, however, is a little more realistic and shows the why behind the ordeal. The basic story is similar: a former Green Beret takes on a small-town police force. This isn't so hard to believe. One man could mess with many small-town sheriff departments. The "why" is what makes the book interesting. In the book, Rambo isn't so innocent. He misses the action of Vietnam, and he doesn't just wound the cops, he kills them. I'm going to ruin the ending for you here. In the end they kill him. Probably a much more realistic ending to that kind of ordeal. Most situations involving violence end rather gruesomely and in manners that are not happy. But then you can't make sequels, so it was changed for the big screen.

The point to all of this is that there are people who become addicted to and like violent encounters. They may not actually like the violence, but they like the feelings that come with it. This, in turn, leads to their wanting to fight. Dad remembers people in Vietnam who didn't leave there because of this. They knew what they were and what they had become, and they didn't want to go back to the States. They chose to remain in the violent world they had grown accustomed and addicted to.

Wanting to fight doesn't automatically make a person bad, even though some people would think so. Remember, some people don't understand this at all. How you handle these feelings determines what kind of person you are.

I haven't always handled these feelings in the best way, even though I always justified my actions to make them seem more appropriate. My father was the same way. Neither of us likes a bully. So, when the feelings of frustration or whatever turned to wanting to pound someone, what could you do? It would be against our beliefs to go and beat someone up for the hell of it or to bully someone.

Unfortunately, there are a lot of people out there who get off by bullying and beating on people who can't fight back. Those are the people I'd look for. If I told some loudmouth to shut up, and instead he started something with me, his loss right? I didn't "start" it, he did. Anyway, I think you see the point.

The problem with these feelings is that violence and fighting can have severe consequences, as has been mentioned throughout this book. That is why you must learn to control these feelings. My father learned how, and so have I. It is difficult at times, and I still do have the feelings. My father still gets them too. It's just that now they are under control.

The first step to overcoming the problem—and it can be a problem—is recognizing the feeling. It can be different in each person, so you need to recognize it in yourself. I've often described it to other people as a huge fire inside me; at times it would feel as if I were going to explode. My dad describes it as a wild animal inside—an animal that you have to keep caged except for in dire emergencies, when it's what will get you out of a situation alive.

However you want to define it, think about the times when its fury has been unleashed and has either gotten you into trouble or saved your hide in a dangerous situation. You see, that animal or fire inside isn't all bad. It can help you if you learn to control it. Control, or mastery of yourself, is the key. And believe me, sometimes it takes a lot to keep it under wraps.

If you know that you have this fire burning inside, the next step is to realize and determine what brings it out. This takes a lot of introspection, but it can be worth the trouble.

Remember, it gets expensive paying for things you break and people you hurt. The ultimate price, of course, is ending up in prison or the morgue because you couldn't control yourself. It was this realization that prompted my dad to gain control of his feelings and to start avoiding confrontations. He sat in the courtroom and realized that things needed to change or everything else he was working toward would be lost. He'd get killed or be on his way to prison if he continued. He tried to teach this to me so I wouldn't end up facing either of those outcomes. Finally, I've reached the same conclusion: control of oneself is important.

Personally, intense frustration and the pain of rejection were the two factors that fueled the fire in me the most. Physical pain was and is much easier for me to deal with than emotional pain. So if I was hurt emotionally, I'd turn to something physical. It was much easier to understand and deal with.

I've learned to recognize when these feelings start to arise, and I turn to other activities to put the fire out before it becomes consuming. Often I need to be alone, or with someone who understands. I have also learned that doing something physical makes it worse. Punching something, lifting something heavy, throwing things, and so on, only intensify the situation and invariably make me madder. I have found I need to do something calming. Again, this works for me, and you'll have to determine what works best for you. The key is to sublimate your energy—direct it toward something positive.

Another good thing is that you will become better at controlling these feelings as you grow older and practice mastery of yourself. Like anything else, it gets easier with practice and time.

You learn this about yourself and you control it, or it will control you. At times, I've felt that maybe because the feeling didn't arise as often, I wouldn't have "the edge" if I really needed it. My father assured me that I shouldn't worry. He's right. The fire or animal will always be there when you need it; you just have to keep it under control until that time comes. And if you are really lucky, that time won't arrive.

REALIZING WHEN YOU DON'T HAVE TO

"As we grow older, we recognize that certain battles are no longer worth fighting. Therefore, we choose our conflicts carefully, just as we choose the road on which we walk with increasing care."

—Denis Waitley

Empires of the Mind

Even though I believe that sometimes you have to fight, I still think people fight many times when they shouldn't or don't have to. You need to recognize that you don't need to fight in all situations and look for and find alternatives. If fighting is an activity you engage in because of stress, you should look for an alternate means of relieving your tensions.

I think a lot of this comes from growing up and wising up with age. But who says you can't wise up sooner? Unfortunately, some never do get a clue and continue down the path of destruction until it's too late. Many wait until something jars them

249

into reality, and they realize just how detrimental their chosen path is. Most people who have been through actual violence learn that it is serious and that there are much better ways to spend your time. Learn from those who have been there and channel your energies into another direction.

I was in a bar in Missouri with Frank about a year ago. We were playing pool and reminiscing about old times. A number of college-age guys were also in the place, drinking and playing pool. Obviously, they hadn't been around much, because they had no poolroom etiquette at all. Frank and I have played in places where acting like them would be a sure way to ensure you'd be carried out of the joint. (Unless you were still conscious, then you'd be tossed out.)

I commented to Frank that one of these days they would be taught a lesson if they ever ventured out into the larger world. Frank replied, "A few years ago you would have been teaching some lessons to them."

"Yeah," I replied. "Don't think I haven't thought about it."

"I know," Frank said. "I've thought about giving that one a good smack upside his head to teach him some manners. But I just don't feel like trouble tonight."

"That's exactly it. I'm just not in the mood for any of that tonight. I don't really feel like going to jail, either," I answered.

"Maybe we're just getting old," Frank joked.

"Maybe," I sighed. "Or maybe we're just growing up."

"Yeah, that's probably it."

It's true—when I was younger, I would have said something about the lack of etiquette and poolroom manners they had. I was real close that night. But there comes a time when you have to realize that you don't need to start things over little insignificant events. Saying something would have only provoked a conflict. I wasn't afraid that Frank and I couldn't handle it, I just didn't want the trouble. I was getting ready to head out to Japan, and I didn't want or need anything to jeopardize that.

I was going through a difficult period a while back and really felt like going out and engaging in a big brawl. Instead, I made a couple of phone calls. One was to my dad. His advice was not to go out and get into trouble. He also said that when you start to get older, your body won't do all the things it did when you were younger. You need to realize this and act accordingly. Maybe that's why we grow up and become smarter. If we don't, our bodies just won't take it. Sure, you can and should stay in good shape so you can do as much as possible. But you're still not going to be able to do the things you could when you were 18 to 25. If you are still in your younger years, you need to consider that the things you do now will catch up with you. I know a lot of people who suffer from injuries that occurred when they were younger. So what about the times when you just want to go cause some trouble? You get these feelings of wanting to smash something or someone.

Actually, these feeling are a form of stress, and there are many ways to deal with these emotions. Find something that works for you. Unfortunately, one of my favorite ways is not always available to me, and it scares some people who don't know me very well. One of my best ways to relax and calm down is by shooting. Living in Montana enables me to go out and shoot just about whenever I want. However, in other places I've lived, areas for shooting haven't been as accessible. Plus, seeing someone upset leaving with a firearm can be disturbing for some people, and justifiably so.

But for me it works. When shooting you learn to be completely relaxed. To put a shot exactly where you want it, you must go into a set routine. There is no room for anything else. So, when I lie down behind a rifle, everything else leaves and it has a calming effect on me. This is a key to managing your violent emotions. Find something calming! If you do something physical, it can just feed the fire. I can remember getting

251

madder when I tried to work out anger by bench pressing and couldn't lift what I wanted. This can be dangerous when you're using weights over 300 pounds.

There is a big difference here in when strenuous exercise can be beneficial and when it just makes things worse. When your feelings are hurt or you're frustrated, a good, hard workout can do tremendous amounts of good. I've gone into the gym after being rejected and lifted till I puked. It helped! It's when you are in the anger stage that something physical can make you worse. When angry, find something that calms you down!

Sometimes I have been known to take out my anger by driving. This is another very dangerous way to vent frustrations. It is dangerous to yourself and anyone else on the road. Don't be stupid behind the wheel. I'm still thankful that I missed the cow that was in the middle of the road the night I was blazing down a backcountry road at night because I was upset. I knew a girl who wasn't so lucky, and she was killed when she rolled her truck while driving angry. When you think about it, driving fast and fighting have similarities. They are both activities that you must concentrate on fully, and there is the element of danger and the adrenaline rush that goes with each. They just aren't good ways to relieve stress. You want something that puts out the fire, not something that fuels it.

Letting a friend know what calms you is also not a bad idea. Friends can help you find the calm in the storm. All one of my friends needs to say to me is, "Would a sniper let anger get in the way of the mission? Does a warrior let anger control him, or does the warrior control his anger?" Find your own control mechanism, and learn to control yourself. There's a time to use anger and the fire inside, and there's a time to keep it tucked away. Letting it go wild whenever and wherever will only land you in trouble. Believe me, I've been in my share of trouble because of a hot temper. I look back now and think, "How stupid, why did it take so long for me to wise up?" I rarely get mad anymore. And when I do, I try to get myself under control as quickly as I can.

Each person will have to learn to control himself. There are a lot of resources out there to help you better yourself. Check these out. A person must always continue to learn and grow. Learn to handle the difficulties in your life in a positive manner. Solve things; don't create new problems by blowing up and saying and doing things you'll regret.

I told Frank about a convention I was going to and what Animal told me. He said he'd take care of the convention and hotel in Las Vegas, but I'd have to pay for my own food, booze, women, and bail. Frank laughed and said, "He knows you pretty well. At least how you were when you were 21."

Yep, that's true, but now I've changed, and I realize when I don't have to fight. I'm ready if I have to; I just hope I can solve any problems that come my way differently. (By the way, I didn't get into any trouble at the convention.)

"Don't mess with the old men; there's a

reason we got to be so old."

—Michael Chiaet,

passing on some

wisdom from his father

I hope this book caused you to think a little about some of the different aspects I discussed. As I said in the beginning, I don't know everything. I didn't even come close to putting everything I know in this book. But I hope what I did write is useful to you.

If you are in the middle of a violent lifestyle, I hope you can find a way out and enjoy the other wondrous things available. If you have never experienced violence, I hope that you never do. I hope you never spend time puking your guts out after some violent encounter. Remember the movie and book *Death Wish*? The first time

255

the hero, Paul Kersey (Paul Benjamin in the book), kills, he goes off to puke. This is more like reality than just blowing someone away.

This book contains just a few of my reflections on some of the things I have done and experienced that may help you grow and better yourself. There are many things that I didn't tell here, but the things I did share teach some of the points I wanted to get across. This book is only another tool for you to use in your own quest for excellence. Take the lessons I have given and adapt them to your own life-style.

Dan Inosanto has one of the greatest book titles ever with his book *Absorb What Is Useful*. This is true with everything. Take the parts of my book and every other book you read, and absorb what is useful to you individually. There is a plaque on the wall of Dan Inosanto's Filipino Kali Academy. It says, "The truth in combat is different for each individual in this style." Then there are four rules, as follows:

1) Research your own experience.
2) Absorb what is useful.
3) Reject what is useless.
4) Add what is specifically your own.

Just reading a book on something won't do you any good unless you use the material. Get out and practice so you will be ready for an encounter if you need to be. But try to use your awareness and avoidance techniques to stay out of trouble.

I'm continuing to learn all of the time as I write, speak, and teach others. My goal is to help as many people as I can and to make the world a better place. This may seem idealistic, but I sincerely believe that the good things you put out will come back to you. So I'll continue to learn about the things in this book as well as the other topics I speak on and write about.

I wasn't joking at the beginning when I said tell me about your mistakes and experiences so we can learn from each other. I believe people are our greatest resource. I'd enjoy talking to you about things in this book or beyond. Write to me in care of Paladin Press, and I'll get back to you.

When I was in the 2nd ID Scout Sniper School, we read where a sniper was often considered a phantom-like creature. From that day, I've been "phantom-like," at least in thought, if not always in action. So I'll say so long with this closing.

—Phantom-like,
Alain

SUGGESTED READING LIST

Here's a list of the books that I have found the most useful in the areas covered in this book. You may want to check them out yourself.

For fighting and survival:

A Bouncer's Guide to Barroom Brawling: Dealing with the Sucker Puncher, Streetfighter, and Ambusher by Peyton Quinn
Cheap Shots, Ambushes, and Other Lessons: A Down and Dirty Book on Streetfighting and Survival by Marc "Animal" MacYoung
Fists, Wits, and a Wicked Right: Surviving on the Wild Side of the Street by Marc "Animal" MacYoung
Floor Fighting: Stompings, Maimings, and Other Things to Avoid When a Fight Goes to the Ground by Marc "Animal" MacYoung

Knives, Knife Fighting, and Related Hassles: How to Survive a Real *Knife Fight* by Marc "Animal" MacYoung

Patton's Principles, by Porter B. Williamson

Pool Cues, Beer Bottles, and Baseball Bats: Animal's Guide to Improvised Weapons for Self-Defense and Survival by Marc "Animal" MacYoung

Principles of Personal Defense by Jeff Cooper

Put 'em Down, Take 'em Out! Knife Fighting Techniques from Folsom Prison by Don Pentecost

Safe in the City: A Streetwise Guide to Avoid Being Robbed, Raped, Ripped Off, or Run Over by Marc "Animal" MacYoung and Chris Pfouts

Street E and E: Evading, Escaping, and Other Ways to Save Your Ass When Things Get Ugly by Marc "Animal" MacYoung

Violence, Blunders, and Fractured Jaws: Advanced Awareness Techniques and Street Etiquette by Marc "Animal" MacYoung

For health and fitness:

The Aerobics Program for Total Well-Being by Kenneth H. Cooper, M.D.

Dr. Bob Arnot's Guide to Turning Back the Clock by Robert Arnot, M.D.

Encyclopedia of Modern Bodybuilding by Arnold Schwarzenegger with Bill Dobbins

The Complete Book of Abs by Kurt Brungardt